ANTICIPATE

ANTICIPATE

KNOWING WHAT CUSTOMERS NEED
BEFORE THEY DO

BILL THOMAS & **JEFF TOBE**

WILEY

JOHN WILEY & SONS, INC.

Cover image: Getty Images / © Rebecca Van Ommen
Cover design: Paul McCarthy

Published by John Wiley & Sons, Inc., Hoboken, New Jersey.
Published simultaneously in Canada.

For general information on our other products and services or for technical support, please contact
our Customer Care Department within the United States at (800) 762-2974, outside the United
States at (317) 572-3993 or fax (317) 572-4002.

Wiley publishes in a variety of print and electronic formats and by print-on-demand. Some material
included with standard print versions of this book may not be included in e-books or in print-on-
demand. If this book refers to media such as a CD or DVD that is not included in the version you
purchased, you may download this material at http://booksupport.wiley.com. For more information
about Wiley products, visit www.wiley.com.

Library of Congress Cataloging-in-Publication Data:

Tobe, Jeff.
    Anticipate : knowing what customers need before they do / Jeff Tobe, Bill Thomas.
      p. cm.
    Includes index.
    ISBN 978-1-118-35691-3 (cloth : alk. paper); ISBN 978-1-118-41721-8 (ebk);
    ISBN 978-1-118-42023-2 (ebk); ISBN 978-1-118-43408-6
      1. Customer relations. 2. Strategic planning. I. Thomas, Bill, 1955– II. Title.
  HF5415.5.T63 2013
  658.8'342—dc23

                                   2012035833

Printed in the United States of America

10 9 8 7 6 5 4 3 2 1

CONTENTS

Strategy—Creating and Destroying Customer Value

- Assess your strategy's potential for success
- Dispel common myths about strategy and its drivers
- Introduce the Customer Focus Framework and Maturity Model

It's estimated that as many as 90 percent of strategies fail to deliver the value or results they were intended to.[1] In most cases, that "value" is generally interpreted to mean shareholder value, return on capital employed, or some other proxy for a predictable and dependable return on investment. Some of those failures are significant, some are modest, and some are incremental—but in all cases, the feeling is . . . they could have done better.

Our experience shows two main reasons why strategies fail to deliver as promised. They were either faulty in design, or they were faulty in implementation. And oftentimes, it's some of both.

---

[1] Scott Glatstein, "Why Strategies Fail: Bridging the Gap between Thinkers and Doers," MWORLD, Fall 2008; The Journal of the American Management Association, Volume 7, Number 3, page 26.

This holds true whether you're trying to develop a broad business strategy or a more specific customer focus strategy. Chances are, if your organization has a formal customer focus strategy, you feel pretty good about its chances for success. And if you personally played a role in designing that strategy, you're most likely feeling quite bullish about it. Let's see. The following pages contain a brief assessment that will give you some insight into what you might realistically expect about your customer focus strategy's likelihood of success.

Assessing Your Strategy's Potential for Success

This self-assessment is meant to help you evaluate the potential for success of your business growth strategy and its underlying customer focus. Generally, the higher your score in a given question or area, the greater potential your organization has of succeeding in its customer focus efforts—thus generating the growth you want from your business strategy.

The thirty (30) questions address various aspects of the Customer Focus Maturity Model® (CFMM) and 10-Point Customer Focus Framework, which will be covered in great detail throughout this book. We've chosen questions that represent a wide range of customer focus critical success factors, but it is not meant to be an exhaustive or all-inclusive list of such questions.

NOTE: There are no right or wrong answers, only the answers that most closely reflect your company's current state. Some of the questions may sound similar, so please read them carefully to understand the difference they're meant to capture. You may struggle a bit on some of them trying to differentiate between a specific department or function in your company and the company as a whole. For this assessment, we are focusing on your company as a whole. Reflect the answer that most closely describes your views about the entire company. Once you have answered all thirty questions, there are instructions at the end of the assessment to help you through the next steps.

To begin, for each question, indicate which answer most appropriately reflects your current view of your company (note we use the term "company" to mean both for-profit and non-profit organizations).

Access this assessment online at www .ANTICIPATEtheExperience.com/assessment or scan the QR code.

Scan for printable copy

ASSESSING YOUR POTENTIAL FOR SUCCESS		
For each statement below, please indicate the number (score) that best reflects your level of agreement or disagreement with each respective statement as follows:		

4 = Strongly Agree	3 = Agree More Than Disagree	2 = Disagree More Than Agree	1 = Strongly Disagree

	Section A Statements	Score
1	Our growth strategy is more about creating value for our customers than it is about creating demand for our offerings.	
2	We are a change leader more than a follower in our key customer markets.	
3	Our customers play a significant role in helping us determine our customer focus philosophy.	
4	We use customer insights to define our definition and measures of strategic success.	
5	Our company views retaining current customers as more important than going after new customers.	
6	We know the average annual profit of each of our customer segments.	
7	We take specific steps to understand how each customer defines value in their relationship with suppliers like us.	
8	We have a formal process for setting and communicating expectations with new customers.	
9	We take specific, consistent steps to understand exactly why customers choose us and why customers leave us.	
10	We identify and focus on all the various touch points in the customer organization.	
	Section A Total Score	

ASSESSING YOUR POTENTIAL FOR SUCCESS			
For each statement below, please indicate the number (score) that best reflects your level of agreement or disagreement with each respective statement as follows:			
4 = Strongly Agree	3 = Agree More Than Disagree	2 = Disagree More Than Agree	1 = Strongly Disagree

	Section B Statements	Score
11	Every employee in our company can describe our customer focus to people outside of our company.	
12	Our employees understand the role the customer plays in the growth and financial success of our company.	
13	Our employees understand how their individual financial well-being and job security depend on our company's success.	
14	Every employee in the company understands the role they play in our customer focus.	
15	Every employee is equipped to play their respective role in our customer focus.	
16	We take clear steps to build customer-focused capabilities throughout the entire company.	
17	"Customer-focused" describes our company culture more than it describes a function or department within our company.	
18	We focus on the entire end-to-end customer experience, not just the sales and service aspects of it.	
19	We have a process in place for ensuring we know what our customers' future needs might be.	
20	Our loyal customers understand what we expect of them in terms of brand advocacy and new business referrals.	
	Section B Total Score	

ASSESSING YOUR POTENTIAL FOR SUCCESS			
For each statement below, please indicate the number (score) that best reflects your level of agreement or disagreement with each respective statement as follows:			
4 = Strongly Agree	3 = Agree More Than Disagree	2 = Disagree More Than Agree	1 = Strongly Disagree

	Section C Statements	Score
21	We execute our strategies far more effectively than our top competitors execute theirs.	
22	We have 3 to 5 key customer-focus measures that are tracked and discussed in every department and at every level of our company.	
23	We are as interested in the success of our customers as we are in our own success.	
24	We focus as sharply on understanding our past customers and future customers as we do on understanding our current customers.	
25	We have a long-term commitment and approach to customer focus.	
26	Our employees are motivated to play their respective roles in our customer focus.	
27	We hire, train, reward, and exit people in a way that supports an effective customer focus.	
28	There are meaningful consequences for the people who fulfill, as well as those who don't fulfill, the role we expect them to play in our customer focus.	
29	We are very effective at identifying and addressing people or units who do not support our customer focus.	
30	We do not tolerate any silo mentality or behavior across our business units or departments.	
	Section C Total Score	
	Grand Total Score (Section A + Section B + Section C)	

Once you've recorded your answer for each of the thirty questions, add up your totals for sections A, B, and C, as well as your Grand Total Score. Then look to the comments below to understand the implications of your ratings.

Questions 1–10 examine the strength of your company's customer-strategy connection and your focus on the unique sources and drivers of customer value as a growth enabler. These questions generally correspond to Level I of the Customer Focus Maturity Model® and tie most closely to steps 1–3 of the Ten-Point Customer Focus Framework.

Questions 11–20 examine the extent to which your people are trained, equipped, and inspired to understand and do their part in creating and leveraging loyal customers. These questions generally correspond to Level II of the Customer Focus Maturity Model® and tie most closely to steps 3–7 of the Ten-Point Customer Focus Framework.

Questions 21–30 examine the steps you take to create a customer-focused culture that consistently generates the mutual profitability of true value chain partnerships. These questions generally correspond to Level III of the Customer Focus Maturity Model® and tie most closely to steps 8–10 of the 10-Point Customer Focus Framework.

Look at your scores for each of the three areas, and see which area(s) you might have the most room for improving relative to another. You can pay particular attention to the relatively weaker area(s) as you proceed through the book.

You can also look at your Grand Total Score. Generally speaking, we find that companies' scores for this assessment correspond to the following maturity levels in the Customer Focus Maturity Model® (CFMM):

Scores Less than 75 = CFMM Level I

Scores Between 75 and 104 = CFMM Level II

Scores Between 105 and 120 = CFMM Level III

Anticipate is about identifying selected customers or customer segments, and taking specific steps to move them along your Customer Focus efforts to increasingly more mature levels; with the ultimate goal of gaining the mutual profitability associated with Level III relationships.

As you'll see in our early discussions, we don't believe a business strategy, if it truly is intended to drive growth and create value, will succeed unless it is built on the design and implementation of a strong customer focus. To better appreciate why and how organizations miss out on creating value, let's look at some commonly held beliefs about the customer–strategy connection.

Debunking Some Key Myths

One thing about commonly held beliefs: They don't always reflect the reality of the situation, or the wisdom to recognize it.

Myth #1: A Strategy Must Inspire Your People

First and foremost, at the heart of, and running throughout, any worthwhile business strategy must be the goal of creating *customer* value. It's not the shareholders, C-level executives, or board members that tell you whether or not your strategy was successful. It's your customers—and the decisions they make each day about your products and services and those of your competitors—that determine your strategy's success. It's those customer decisions that translate into sales, profits, and your ultimate return on investment. A good strategy must and should inspire your people—but it first must inspire your customers to act. If it doesn't, then you end up with an inspired organization that isn't as successful as it wants to be. If your desired end state is to be happy or inspired, regardless of your business's success, then you don't need a strategy. It's pretty easy to end up happy, but broke.

To make customers act, an effectively designed strategy must recognize that growth isn't about finding new customers for your products and services as much as it is about finding new ways to create value for your customers (both existing and prospective customers). That value often comes from being able to identify and meet the customers' unmet, unstated, and unknown needs better than, or before, your competitors do. And that ability comes from building and leveraging a relationship and sense of partnership with a customer that uniquely positions you to anticipate future value streams that mutually profit both sides.

Myth #2: Not All Strategies Produce Change

They better! If they don't . . . why bother?

Without getting bogged down in theory or academic definitions, a strategy is about the decisions an organization makes, that when implemented, create the most value over time. Strategies are about creating new, more productive, faster or cheaper, more unique, or more sustainable sources of value. Their core purpose is to create a future state that's better than the current state. They are every bit about change!

And that is precisely one of the reasons strategies often fail or underperform in implementation. Companies fail to recognize the extent to which a strategy requires change—change in culture, change in leadership practices, change in customer-facing processes, change in customer decisions, change in employee behaviors, change in business systems, and so forth. Strategies are about anticipating where the next value-creating opportunities might be in the marketplace, determining what changes the company might have to make to exploit those opportunities, and then ensuring the company has the capabilities needed to execute them effectively. We'll spend a significant amount of time understanding and addressing the change factors—both those that accelerate and those that frustrate—in the implementation of an otherwise sound growth strategy.

Myth #3: Strategies Must Be Achievable

Unfortunately, many organizations first determine what they can afford, or what their current capabilities are, and then use those parameters to shape (limit) their strategic ambitions and choices. So "achievable" often first becomes a question of being affordable or readily doable. We disagree with that thinking in two very important respects.

First of all, no strategy should be developed in a vacuum. A company's financial capacity must certainly be a key consideration because no company has enough money to tackle all the things they want to tackle at a given point in time. There's only so much money to go around. But too often the financial considerations come into play before the rigorous market considerations, or they're considered simultaneously. Either way, the outcome is usually a strategy that was based more on affordability than on market opportunity.

An effectively designed strategy must first be based on an unrestricted, blue-sky search for the most promising market opportunities or investment options we might pursue. Some of those options might be totally out of reach financially, but they should still be on the long list of strategic possibilities. Once that long list is developed, then financial considerations can come into play to help prioritize which of the options on the long list we can afford to pursue. It's a cart-before-the-horse kind of situation. We shouldn't look at what we can afford first and then look for options that fit within those financial parameters. We should develop our list of most optimal options first, and then see which ones we can afford—which ones have the most favorable cost-benefit value. It might seem like a play on words, but it's a very real and significant mindset that can mean the difference between a breakthrough strategy and a benign strategy. (See Figure 1.1.)

Secondly, we agree a strategy must be doable, but we also believe it must represent some degree of stretch. It's better to achieve 80 percent of a strategy that dramatically changes the game for your company or your industry, than to achieve 100 percent of a strategy that creates only modest or minimal change or improvements in your results. If you aim high in your growth goals, you may or may not get there. But if you aim low, you certainly won't get there. Too many companies talk about game-changing results but settle for incremental tactics or initiatives when building their strategy.

There are many possible reasons companies end up creating a strategy that lacks sufficient stretch. One of the more common ones we see is fear of missing your strategic targets. Sentiments that we've heard in more than one strategic planning meeting often sound something like this: *Let's set ourselves up for success and commit to strategic goals that we know we can hit.* Who would argue the logic of that? We would!

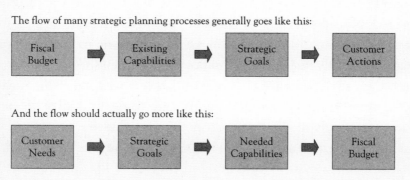

Figure 1.1   **Improving the Flow of Strategic Planning**

In 2000, a popular movie, *The Patriot*, portrayed selected battles of the American Revolutionary War. In one scene, a Continental solider and two of his young sons are staging an ambush of British soldiers. His instructions to his sons, each armed with musket in hand, was "aim small—miss small."

Similarly, when it comes to a company's customer focus, far too many companies also aim small. They settle for the low-hanging fruit. Things like customer service skills and recovery techniques, voice of the customer (VOC) programs, customer satisfaction measures (CSM), or loyalty metrics such as net promoter scores (NPS) and others—while playing an important and valuable role—are small hits that usually yield small or incremental wins.

As we'll discuss, an organization's ability to achieve great things with its strategy will depend on its willingness to commit to a customer focus that stretches well beyond these and other incremental steps.

Myth #4: Strategy Defines a Desired State or Vision

This myth is somewhat viable but not sufficiently true. The business journals are stacked high with examples of strategies having a compelling vision or desired state but where that vision was only partly or minimally achieved. Just as important as that desired state or vision, if not more important, is that a strategy must also define a roadmap for reaching that end state. We're continually surprised by the number of times an executive team will think their strategic planning job is done because they have fully vetted, defined, and justified the company's strategic direction. Then they mistakenly assume they can just "turn it over" to the next level of management to implement it. Effective planners must also focus on the doing, or execution phase, of their strategy. Similarly, those who will be tasked with managing the execution should have involvement in the defining and planning of it. Far too often, those who plan and those who execute are separated by two discrete processes. An effective strategy should focus on implementation as much as it focuses on planning.

The same challenge often exists in the company's customer focus. We have seen numerous companies launch a specific customer-centric practice or an initiative du jour only to see it die on the vine. Among the myriad reasons or causes for false starts or short-lived initiatives, common causes typically include:

- Not engaging the customer *before* designing and/or launching the initiative.
- Not ensuring everyone internally is aligned and equally motivated to support it.
- Not knowing what to do with the results or not having a longer-term plan or process in place for continually leveraging the effort.
- Not anticipating or dealing with the types of resistance or obstacles one might encounter.

These so-called execution derailers create problems that many companies don't anticipate and can't overcome or effectively manage. As a result, implementation of their customer-centric initiative, or their strategy in general, fails or falls short. In sum, you need a solid customer focus to shape and drive your strategy, and you need to be a great implementer of both.

Any source of competitive advantage that is not based on doing something truly unique, wonderful, and imaginative for customers, is simply going to disappear.
—Gary Hamel, named by Fortune *magazine as "the world's leading expert on business strategy"*

Customer Focus—One Part Plan, One Part Roadmap

An effective business strategy must first and foremost inspire your customers to act. It must produce a change inside and outside that is more valuable to your customers than the current state. It must represent an achievable stretch. And it must include both the desired new end state, as well as a path for getting there.

Over the years, we have come to recognize that any customer-centric business strategy generating any amount of success has contained the same 10 key elements. These 10 elements have proven to be critical for both effective design and effective implementation. And the degree of success for a given organization's strategy depends on two variables around these key elements. Those two variables are:

1. The time it takes the company to see the value of and effectively develop and implement each of the 10 elements
2. The degree to which all 10 elements are aligned with each other and aligned with the rest of the business

In the chapters to come, we'll use our 10-Point Customer Focus Framework to illustrate the key steps, techniques, and examples companies use in each element to create a clear and compelling linkage between their customer focus and broader growth strategy. This framework, in effect, provides the template for a solid customer focus plan.

The 10 elements are presented in Figure 1.2. We have listed them in the most logical order such that each subsequent element builds on the prior one. Please note, however, that in practice we have seen many different sequences followed. We have even seen some

TEN-POINT CUSTOMER FOCUS FRAMEWORK	
1. Strategic Drivers	6. Process Orientation
2. Customer Segmentation	7. Joint Workouts
3. Customer Engagement	8. Capacity for Change
4. Employee Engagement	9. Consequences
5. Training & Tools	10. Committed Leadership

Figure 1.2   10-Point Framework for Customer Focus

companies try to skip one or two particular steps—only to learn a tough lesson from it later down the road. More on some of those lessons later.

As for that roadmap we've been placing so much emphasis on, a company typically goes through different stages or levels of success in terms of implementing its customer-centric strategies. Using our Customer Focus Maturity Model® (CFMM), we'll show you the three main stages (maturity levels) of that implementation journey, the tips and traps (lessons learned) of each stage, and suggested techniques and examples to move the organization from one stage (or level) to the next. The basic version of the CFMM is shown in Figure 1.3.

Our CFMM is based on more than two decades of working with various organizations in the design and implementation of their customer-focused strategies. It is based on the efforts, results, and learning of those organizations over time and describes the path or journey most organizations take as they seek to put customers first among their business priorities. The model is used to identify the

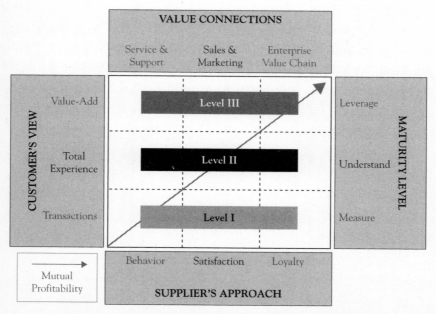

Figure 1.3   Customer Focus Maturity Model®

drivers, opportunities, and techniques needed to increasingly optimize an organization's customer-centric strategy by continually progressing until they reach Level III, which represents optimal profitability for both customer and supplier.

The model uses four dimensions to define the customer–supplier relationship: the supplier's approach to the relationship; the customer's view of the value provided by the supplier; the types of customer–supplier connections involved; and the supplier's maturity level in terms of leveraging the total relationship into mutual profit growth.

The model uses three maturity levels (Levels I, II, and III) to describe and evaluate the techniques used in, and the interactions between, each of the four dimensions—and the resultant impact on mutual profitability at each level.

Our ultimate goal is to show you the benefits of and the way to achieve a Level III customer focus. This is the level where your organization operates as an end-to-end process that exists for one sole purpose: to anticipate, deliver, and profit from creating customer value. A level where everyone in every function is aligned—from the executive level to the entry level—and from employees who face the customer to employees whose faces you never see, around that one common purpose: developing a culture that connects the things going on inside your company to the things going on outside—both with your customers and your suppliers—to create a new way of viewing and leveraging your entire value chain.

Both the 10-Point Customer Focus Framework and the Customer Focus Maturity Model® will be used to guide us through the planning, design, and effective implementation of a truly customer-centric business strategy. As such, we will move back and forth between the two models frequently, showing how and when companies deploy a part of the framework to improve a certain level of customer-focus maturity or how they apply it to get to the next level of maturity. In general, the two models map together as shown in Figure 1.4.

LINKING THE CUSTOMER FOCUS MATURITY MODEL® & FRAMEWORK			
CFMM LEVEL	FRAMEWORK STEP	CFMM LEVEL	FRAMEWORK STEP
I	1. Strategic Drivers	II	6. Process Orientation
↓	2. Customer Segmentation	↓ III	7. Joint Workouts
	3. Customer Engagement		8. Capacity for Change
II	4. Employee Engagement		9. Consequences
↓	5. Training & Tools	↓	10. Committed Leadership

Figure 1.4   Two Models for a Customer-Centric Business Strategy

In the next chapter we will begin with the strategic drivers that should, but too often don't, form the basis of starting any customer-centric strategy or initiative.

CHAPTER 2

Doing the Right Things for the Wrong Reasons

- Link customer focus and your growth strategy
- Differentiate between customer behavior, satisfaction, and loyalty
- Determine the metrics that matter the most

Interest in, support of, and resistance to customer focus can come from any number of places in a company. Just looking at the range of inquiries and requests we receive about it, we note that sometimes the interest comes from a CEO, an executive director, or a COO who wants to increase a business's customer intimacy to grow sales, membership, or gross margin. Other times the interest might come from a senior sales leader (e.g., a sales VP, a sales GM, or a regional sales director) who is concerned about customer retention or account penetration rates, or from a chief marketing officer (CMO) who is trying to advance the organization's brand or understand and improve its win-loss rates in new customer bids, proposals, and tenders. And yet in other situations, the impetus might come from the head of customer service or customer care, or even from a chief customer experience officer (CXO) who wants to get better traction and broader company-wide involvement in the company's customer experience campaign.

No matter how they frame their initial questions, or what they describe as their respective reason for thinking about customer focus, the conversation with each of these different players must eventually get back to the same initial fundamental questions: *What is the strategic benefit of focusing on the customer? How does this customer focus you're asking about help you shape, drive, or support your business strategy?* You would be surprised at how few of them think in these terms. That's why the Customer Focus Framework starts with strategic drivers. If you are pursuing customer focus for the sake of happier customers, or because you instinctively feel it is the right thing to do, you're going to come up short. Here's an actual example that happens more often than you might think.

10-Point Customer Focus Framework

#1. Strategic Drivers

Several years ago, we were contacted by a chief commercial officer (CCO) who was very perplexed and frustrated by his company's performance in its industry's customer satisfaction rating indices. For three years running, the company's performance against benchmark peers had been slipping, and it got to the point that competitors were starting to use the survey results to their advantage (and to the disadvantage of this CCO's company). He wanted us to launch a separate survey process—specifically for his company—that would help identify and resolve customer satisfaction issues *before* the next industry survey was conducted. The results he ultimately wanted were to see his company rising again in the industry-wide survey.

In one of our early meetings with the CCO and his team, we probed to really understand the business reasons for focusing on this survey. From their responses, it was clear that the survey was quite visible and highly relied on by the major players in his industry. It was also clear that he and his team had been very embarrassed when a customer confronted their CEO about the survey results—even though that particular customer hadn't responded to the survey. Finally, they knew that some of their key competitors were getting great publicity, and, they assumed, market leverage by having a formal customer focus or customer experience (CE) campaign or process.

We persisted with our questioning. What is your business reason for doing this? What business results do you expect to gain from it? Their answers continued to focus on perceptions, reputation, bragging rights, and other anecdotal or subjective reasons. They even used the term *competitive advantage* but weren't able to describe what that looked like for them or how it related to the survey. Finally, we pushed the issue by saying: "So if we are able to get your ratings up in the industry-wide satisfaction survey, but your revenues or profits or market share actually go down, will you be happy?" They ultimately got our point. Customer focus has to be grounded in or explicitly linked to your business or growth strategy goals. Happy customers or better ratings aren't the end game we're after. What we're after is a happiness or better ratings that drive customer actions—actions that have an economic benefit for us (revenue growth, market share growth, margin improvement, etc.).

Addressing the Priority Predicament

One other essential reason why any customer focus effort must be tied to your strategy is something we call, for lack of a better term, the *priority predicament*. Michael Dell, the founder and CEO of the personal computer giant Dell Inc., once told a group of his managers that one of the hardest parts of strategic planning isn't choosing the things you'll do, it's choosing the things you won't do. Organizations are usually pretty good at coming up with new initiatives and new priorities. But they aren't particularly good at killing off initiatives that aren't progressing as planned or aren't as important as they once were. The net result is that priorities continue to accumulate to the point where there's so many that to call any of them a priority would be a serious misnomer.

When it comes to introducing a customer focus initiative or process, the natural reaction is for people to see it as a new priority—a layer of work that is being added on to their already full plates. *"I already have my own job keeping me busy 80 hours a week, and now you're asking me to spend time on this customer program?"* You can hear it echoing through the halls right now—in your own organization—can't you? The point is, customer focus can't be an added layer of work; instead, it must be an inherent part of everyone's already existing work. It can't be something we do in addition to our normal job. It must be our normal job. It must be part of our normal job that we do better, or do differently, to enhance its impact on the customer's experience. Getting to that point depends on culture to a large extent, a topic we'll talk about in our Level III discussions. The other part of it is that people must be able to clearly see the customer–strategy connection so they view customer focus not as a new priority, but as a process for aligning and achieving already existing business priorities.

Here is an exercise (see Figure 2.1) we often use when helping management teams better understand this connection. The left column lists 20 common reasons (factors) for having a formal or structured customer focus. The middle column has participants check those economic outcomes impacted by the 20 common reasons. (The items listed in each of these two columns are the ones we use most frequently, but they can be changed to better suit the unique goals or challenges of a given company). And the last column asks them to rank how important each of the 20 reasons is to the organization's strategy or business goals. (Similarly, any number of different ranking scales can be used.) Access the Customer Strategy Connection online at

Scan for printable copy

www.ANTICIPATEtheExperience.com/strategy or scan the QR code.

Sometimes we use it as a questionnaire for managers or leaders to complete and compare results with one another. Other times, we use it as a discussion guide and facilitate a rigorous group conversation about it. There are no right or wrong answers per se. The understanding comes more from the related dialogue and debate. Whether or not the participants agree on every factor doesn't matter. By the time the discussion is over, most participants will see or appreciate the connection between the customer focus and the company's business goals.

Column I Customer Focus Factors	Column II Indicators Impacted				Column III Strategy Importance		
	A	B	C	D	X	Y	Z
INSTRUCTIONS: • For each of the Customer Focus Factors 1 – 20 below, check which items (A – D) in Column II are impacted by each factor. Check all that apply. • Given your thoughts about columns I and II, indicate in Column III how important you think each factor is to your company's business strategy or goals. Check only one (X, Y, or Z).	Revenue	Margin	Share	Productivity	Very Important	Somewhat Important	Not Very Important
1. Forums or venues for customers to vent							
2. Customer problem identification and resolution tool							
3. Identify customer service skill or training issues/needs							
4. Identify communications or policy issues							
5. Identify segment and/or channel issues							
6. Determine customer purchase drivers							
7. Enhance customer retention rates							
8. Increase customer referrals for new business							
9. Increase customer repeat purchases/business							
10. Test our brand promise or value proposition							
11. Generate higher customer satisfaction or loyalty							
12. Lower customer acquisition costs or improve win rates							
13. Increase our share of the customer's spend							
14. Identify our differentiators in the market place							
15. Sell more total solutions/bundled solutions							
16. Identify process issues or improvements							
17. Spawn product/service innovations or enhancements							
18. Increase number of enterprise global or MSA accounts							
19. Develop more collaborative relationships and processes							
20. Create game-changing market drivers or offerings							

Figure 2.1   Customer–Strategy Connection Exercise

Note: Periodically, we'll add a Column IV to the above worksheet, which we label as Strategic Initiatives, or we'll replace Strategy Importance in Column III with Strategic Initiatives. We also provide the participants with a list of the company's current strategic initiatives—each one designated by a unique identifier tag or code. Then we ask participants to identify which Strategic Initiatives are directly impacted by each factor in Column I.

The Customer–Strategy Connection Exercise can be very revealing and very important in your early efforts to help people understand the business drivers behind your customer focus. It forces people to think more deeply about the tangible impact of an initiative they might otherwise consider to be soft, intangible, or unnecessary. This is a common and significant perception gap in many organizations, and it most likely exists in yours although it might not feel that way to you just yet. But in the many surveys, assessments, and focus groups we conduct in various companies, it's clear that the vast majority of managers and employees don't know anything about the following:

- The average cost of a customer complaint
- The average revenue of a lost customer
- The top five reasons why customers defect
- The average sales costs of acquiring a new customer
- The average annual revenue and/or profit per customer
- The lifetime value of an average customer
- The company's win–loss ratio on new prospect bids and proposals
- The top five reasons behind those wins and losses

Can your managers or employees answer the above questions for your organization? Do they care about those questions or answers? Without this basic grounding in the customer-driven income and expense variables, it can be difficult getting people to see the economic, more tangible aspects of focusing on the customer.

Differentiating Customer Behavior, Satisfaction, and Loyalty

Another important aspect of this customer–strategy connection challenge is recognizing the difference between customer behavior, satisfaction, and loyalty, and how each one impacts the company's top and bottom lines. Those differences and impacts will also be key to understanding the customer focus journey using the roadmap of the Customer Focus Maturity Model (CFMM), which we'll be describing later. Here's a relatable personal story that nicely illustrates the difference.

Just a mile down the road from my house is a drugstore. It's the only drugstore in our area that has a drive-through prescription window that is open late at night—even on weekends: a truly great feature if you just can't get to the drugstore during normal business hours, or you have a sick child and need a prescription filled late at night. It's also good because you don't have to get out of the car in bad weather—which is when most of the prescriptions in our house seem to run out and need to be filled.

However, all other features of this particular store are not so appealing. The store shelves and all of the products on those shelves usually have a year's worth of dust on them. And that proverbial "spill in aisle nine" we often hear about on TV commercials . . . well, it's *still* there. And this store's clerks are about as friendly and approachable as . . . okay, you get the picture. The point? When we need a late night prescription run—it's the place we always go. But it's the last place we'll go if we need anything else. In fact, we'll drive miles out of our way or go without something before we'll subject ourselves to the unpleasant experience of visiting that particular store.

In this example (Figure 2.2), our behavior as a customer, given that we might go there several times a year, would lead one to believe we are a satisfied customer—because we keep coming back for more. And when someone in our neighborhood or someone visiting us asks where they can get an after-hours prescription filled, we quickly refer them to

COMMON CUSTOMER CHARACTERISTICS		
Behavior	Satisfaction	Loyalty
Price or convenience	Still price or convenience	Seeks value foremost
Transaction-based	Competitive-based	Engagement-based
Past experience means little	Absence of major negatives	Connections create barriers

Figure 2.2   Comparing Customer Behavior, Satisfaction, and Loyalty

you-know-where. We give that drugstore repeat business, and we give them referral business. Does that make us a satisfied, maybe even loyal, customer? Not at all. The way a customer behaves is not necessarily an indicator of how satisfied they are, or whether they'll increase their spending with you, or promote your brand to others, or how likely they are to not buy from your competitors. Behavior, satisfaction, and loyalty are very different concepts with very different impacts on revenue and profits. Let's look at these general differences and implications.

Typical customers recognize little, if any, differentiation from one supplier to another. Despite differences in quality, service, reliability, or other variables, their buying decisions tend to be driven by price (the cheapest) or convenience (the quickest). Beyond price or convenience, typical customer behavior doesn't consider or respond to much more than that—it's simply a transaction they need or want to complete as painlessly as possible. Even the fact that they may have had a particularly bad experience with you won't necessarily stop them from buying from you again. Conversely, even if they've had a particularly great experience with you, it doesn't mean they won't buy the cheapest or closest solution they can find—from someone else.

Satisfied customers are somewhat better, though in our view not much! They still tend to respond mostly to price or convenience, and while they might not be as quick to buy cheap, they will make some effort to compare prices or fees to see if they can do better (i.e., cheaper) than you. Satisfied customers represent a real blind spot for many companies who conduct customer satisfaction surveys of any type. Lulled into a false sense of comfort by seemingly high satisfaction ratings, these blind-sided companies are often shocked when a "satisfied" customer goes elsewhere. In fact, some research shows that 60–80 percent of defecting customers claim to be satisfied or very satisfied on surveys completed just prior to defecting.[1] In essence, when a customer is satisfied, it simply suggests an absence of negatives in their experience with you. It does not suggest any presence of positives or factors that will consistently drive them your way.

That's why we believe loyalty must be the ultimate goal of any customer experience or customer focus effort. When we say "loyalty," we're not talking about frequent flyer, bonus awards, or other perks customers get for giving a company their repeat business or referring other customers to them. By loyal, we mean the customer sees unique value in the product or service they get from you. This value is so important to them that they are less sensitive to price and convenience, and still buy from you even though you may not be the cheapest or quickest solution around. The loyal customers we seek are the kind of customers who:

- Come exclusively to you to buy a given product or service.
- Are receptive to new product/service releases from you based on their prior experience with you.
- Are quick to refer other prospective customers to you.
- Actively promote (talk positively about) your brand in the marketplace.
- Value their relationship with you and view you as a partner, not just as a supplier or vendor.
- Forgive you for making a mistake or two, rather than abandoning you for a competitor.
- Won't consider a competitor unless forced to and will likely give you a "last look" before making a decision to go to a competitor.

---

[1] Frederick F. Reichheld, *The Loyalty Effect: The Hidden Fact Behind Growth, Profits, and Lasting Value* (Boston: Harvard Business Review Publishing, 2001), 237.

COMMON CUSTOMER RESPONSES		
Unsatisfied Customer	**Satisfied Customer**	**Loyal Customer**
Tolerates you	Prefers you	Insists on you
Goes out of their way to speak negatively about you	Will give their opinion about you but only if asked	Goes out of their way to say great things about you
Tells at least 3 to 5 other current or potential customers*	Their opinion is usually neutral or so non-committal that it leaves doubt	Tells at least 1 to 3 other current or potential customers*

*These are conservative estimates, given our experience. Some experts cite much larger figures than these.

Figure 2.3   Benefits of Loyal Customer Response

That loyalty is what we seek in Level III, and we will discuss it again later. Figure 2.3 points to some other benefits a company gains by shifting its focus from behavior to satisfaction to loyalty.

At least from a qualitative perspective, the impact of having a customer who is unsatisfied, satisfied, or loyal is easy to see. But there are quantitative impacts as well. This book is not meant to present an economic argument in support of customer focus, as there are myriad other resources available that address that. (See sidebar titled *Why Loyal Customers Are More Profitable*.) But based on our experience and a number of other respected works on the subject, there are clear economic differences between satisfied and loyal customers, which are presented in Figure 2.4.

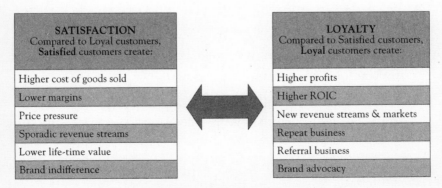

SATISFACTION Compared to Loyal customers, **Satisfied** customers create:		LOYALTY Compared to Satisfied customers, **Loyal** customers create:
Higher cost of goods sold		Higher profits
Lower margins		Higher ROIC
Price pressure		New revenue streams & markets
Sporadic revenue streams		Repeat business
Lower life-time value		Referral business
Brand indifference		Brand advocacy

Figure 2.4   Satisfaction versus Loyalty

Why Loyal Customers Are More Profitable

Frederick F. Reichheld, author of *The Loyalty Effect*, found that the economic benefits of customer loyalty compound over time. While the loss of one or more customers may not have a significant or persuasive impact on the current year's profits, even small changes in customer retention (loyalty) can permeate a business system and multiply as years accumulate. Figure 2.5 illustrates the incremental gains that mount over time as a customer stays with a supplier year after year.

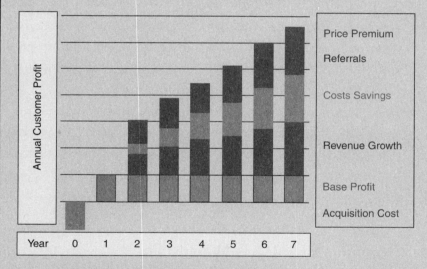

Figure 2.5 Benefits of Customer Loyalty Accrue over Time

Frederick F. Reichheld, *The Loyalty Effect: The Hidden Fact Behind Growth, Profits, and Lasting Value* (Boston: Harvard Business Review Publishing, 2001).

Basic explanations of the terms used in Figure 2.5 are below.

- Acquisition Cost: In general the one-time cost of attracting and closing on a new customer, which may include advertising, sales commissions or incentives, sales force overhead, and so forth.

- Base Profit: The price customers pay in addition to the company's cost is the base profit. The base profit on basic purchases generally is not affected by time, loyalty, efficiency, or other factors.

- Revenue Growth: In most businesses, customer spending tends to accelerate over time as the result of the customer's repeat business, using competitors less, and being more receptive to new product/service introductions.

- Cost Savings: Relationships become more efficient over time, as each side learns how to most effectively do business with the other. Existing relationships require less sales effort (and costs).

- Referrals: The more consistently customers are satisfied by a given supplier, the more likely they are to refer other prospects to that supplier; and customer referrals tend to be prequalified prospects.

- Price Premiums: Longer-term customers usually don't need special deals and discounts to stay with a supplier the way new prospects do to go with a supplier. In general, the more value a customer receives over time, the less sensitive they are to general price increases or value-based pricing.

Don't Measure What You Can—Measure What Matters

One remaining aspect of the strategy-customer connection we want to discuss is metrics. There are two key points we want to make in this section about the metrics companies use to track, prioritize, and manage their customer focus efforts. The first point relates back to our chief commercial officer (CCO) mentioned in Chapter 1 who wanted his own customer satisfaction measurement (CSM) survey process to augment or refute the broader industry-wide survey that had been hurting his company in the marketplace. As you'll recall, we had to push him and his senior management team to think about what they were really after with this survey, and what measures were most important to them. As the old adage goes: *You can't manage what you don't measure.* But we have found another related concept to be equally true: *You'll only get what you DO measure.* In the case of our CCO, it meant that even if the company sought an improved customer satisfaction measurement (CSM) score, they really wouldn't be happy if it didn't translate into measurable top-line or bottom-line improvements.

We see many customer focus efforts lose their momentum, credibility, or support because they only monitor and talk about what we view as *intermediate measures.* Metrics like customer satisfaction measures, loyalty indexes, net promoter scores, customer referral numbers, brand strength or awareness metrics, retention rates, win–loss ratios, and the like are all very important for evaluating the progress you're making and determining where adjustments are needed. And while C-level leaders intuitively understand the importance of them, the metrics don't always influence these executives. They are more influenced by *ultimate measures* like revenues, profits, market share, and return on investments (ROI). That's why, as much as possible, companies try to calculate, demonstrate, or at least articulate the linkage between those customer focus intermediate measures and ultimate financial measures. For example:

- Knowing that the customer turnover rate is 15 percent isn't quite as compelling as combining that with the fact that each customer account lost last year was worth an average of $80,000 per year.

- Knowing that each customer complaint hurts our brand and increases customer turnover risks isn't as compelling as knowing we spend an average of $6,000 following up on each type AA complaint and for every 10 class AA complaints—we lose one customer.

- Knowing that it's easier to sell to an existing customer than it is to acquire a new customer is a given. But knowing that it costs an average of $30,000 to win a new account versus $7,500 to sell more business to an existing account is far more persuasive.

- Knowing that our new bid win–loss ratio is 4:1 is important. However, it's even more meaningful to know that the average amount of each bid won was $65,000, and the average amount of each lost bid was $90,000.

- Knowing the average profit per customer isn't as meaningful as also knowing what the average profit per customer segment is.

Customer focus measures are important. They're even more important when they are considered and discussed in conjunction with the ultimate financial indicators they affect.

The second key point about using metrics that matter relates to what the customer views as important. We are often called in to a client situation to evaluate, improve, or totally rebuild their customer satisfaction or loyalty measurement process. One of the first questions we typically ask is: *What role did your customers play in helping you to develop your current survey process?* This question generates a blank stare more often than one might think. So the next question we ask is: *How do you know you're surveying your customers about factors they view as important?* More blank stares! The truth is that many companies assume they know what is important to their customers. They assume they know what the customer views as a minor glitch, versus a troubling concern, versus a deal breaker. But too many times the company's assumptions are inaccurate.

In one particular case, a company had a survey process that had been in place for about four years. While managers were seeing incremental improvement in the company's satisfaction scores, they weren't seeing any real improvements in margin growth per account, new product/service penetration of existing accounts, or customer retention and referral results. The current CSM survey tool, which was concise and easy to complete, asked customers for their views in five key areas (see Figure 2.6).

We made two small changes to their existing CSM tool. First, we added a sixth line for the customer to write in any other (up to three more) factors that were important to them in addition to the

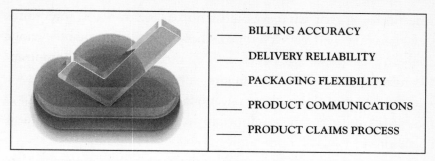

	BILLING ACCURACY
	DELIVERY RELIABILITY
	PACKAGING FLEXIBILITY
	PRODUCT COMMUNICATIONS
	PRODUCT CLAIMS PROCESS

Figure 2.6   One Company's Satisfaction Metrics

five already listed. Second, we added a column for the customer to also rank how important each of the five existing factors were to them, as well as a rank for any write-in factors they added. The results were very insightful.

These three new factors were added by a significant number of responding customers:

_____ CONTRACTING (Terms and Conditions)

_____ VALUE FOR PRICE

_____ MISSING, WRONG, OR DAMAGED PARTS

As for the rankings of importance, billing accuracy and delivery reliability were seldom among the top five in importance in the customers' views. They were viewed as givens or nonnegotiables. The customers did not view them as differentiators. The customers felt that if bills weren't accurate or deliveries weren't provided as promised, they wouldn't be doing business with the company at all. Billing accuracy and delivery reliability were binary factors. Either you do them well or you don't—no grades or shades in between. Good to know!

To further compound this disconnect, many times companies get a survey process in place and then, to ensure they have some continuity on the survey tool that makes year-to-year comparisons possible, they leave the survey tool untouched for several years in a row.

The reality is that what was most important to a customer three years ago may well have changed since then. But the survey tool a company uses does not necessarily change. So it's very important to engage a sampling of customers before designing a survey tool, and then to recalibrate them periodically to ensure the survey still measures the things most important to them. We'll talk a bit more about survey tools and processes in our Level I discussions.

CHAPTER 3

Not All Customers Are Good Customers

- Segment your customer base to sharpen and guide your focus
- Realize the ultimate goal is mutual profitability
- Start the customer focus journey (the Customer Focus Maturity Model®)

Effective implementation of a customer-focused strategy takes courage to start, persistence to stay the course despite setbacks, and an unyielding drive to achieve Level III's mutual profitability outcome. It is not for the faint of heart and it's not the right approach for all of your customers. To put this last comment in perspective, let's look at three typically held beliefs about customer focus and what's wrong with each of them.

1. The customer is always right.
2. Whatever it takes—keep them satisfied.
3. All customers are important.

First of all, customers are *not* always right. They are just as capable of making a mistake as any supplier is. Whether they agree or not, they are also partly responsible for ensuring the customer–supplier relationship is successful. Part of a sustained successful relationship is continually educating each other on what each side needs from the other to make it work, and how each can continually improve the efficacy of their respective roles. That means—at times—letting each other know when they've made a mistake or have caused a misstep in the process.

While most companies totally get it when it comes to getting tough feedback from their customers, most of them are uncomfortable with the reverse—providing tough feedback *to* the customer. The fact is that periodically a company does have to set the customer straight on some things. Disagreeing with a customer or showing them how they could have done something better is not inherently a bad thing to do. When problems arise, however, they involve the ways in which something is done. The timing, tone, choice of words, communication tool used, and the particular players involved—both on the sending and receiving end—can mean the difference between a productive or destructive communications exchange.

Providing feedback to the customer is something companies need to be (or get) comfortable doing. Each time the company misses or ignores an opportunity to help the customer learn or improve, it makes the next instance even that much harder to effectively address. Before too long, the relationship has become painfully one-sided. They're always right and you're always wrong.

The notion of "whatever it takes" is similarly a problem. It denies the very fact of why companies have customers in the first place. Hopefully, that reason is to make money. When companies say, *keep the customer satisfied no matter what it takes*, it implies they'll take a loss (tangible or intangible) if they have to—just to keep customers happy. But that approach, as noble and customer-focused as it seems, ignores the company's need to make a profit. There must be limits on the extent to which a company will bend (or the money it will forgo or spend) to satisfy a customer. It also ignores the fact that there are some customers out there who are bullies—plain and simple. They intimidate, threaten, and criticize a supplier to the point where the supplier's margins are razor thin or their employees run for cover every time the customer calls or visits. Bully customers can be toxic to a company's economics and to a company's employees. We've all seen them and we've all seen companies tolerate them. You must have a reasonable line that you won't cross and will effectively tell the customer: *Enough is enough. We've run out of options. We can't give in or give up any more and still make sense of this relationship or particular deal. The only way we can continue making this work is if you (our customers) agree to do so and so.*

This is also an important message for your customer-facing employees to understand. When employees feel their company will always give in, they lose pride and confidence in the company's leadership, value, and brand. It shows in their behavior both at work and outside of work. On the other hand, there's a visible sense of pride, shared purpose, and advocacy in employees who know their company will stand up to unreasonable customers, manage customers' unrealistic expectations, and enjoy a mutually rewarding relationship with their customers. Again, the ways in which these things are done (through tone, approach, words, timing, and the like) will be the key to taking a firm but successful stand when you need to.

The third and equally important belief is that all customers are important. In many respects this is absolutely true. All customers are important in terms of the continued business they give you, the referral business they send your way, and the way they talk about you in the marketplace. But that doesn't mean they are all equally important. Some customers cost you more to supply (lower margins), generate smaller revenue streams for you (refer less new business your way, buy relatively less from you, or buy less frequently from you), and create more intangible costs for you (high-maintenance relationships, brand-weakening behaviors).

This is where the lifetime value (LTV) of a customer can come into play. Ideally, you want all customers to be as profitable to you as possible and stay with you forever. So it's important to look at the total value (revenue from and cost of servicing) of an account over time. For example, it might seem like a customer that buys $250,000 of product or service from you every 5 years is less important to you than a customer who buys $75,000 from you every year for a 10-year period. Add to that the fact that the $75K/year customer is very hard to do business with, entails much higher transaction costs for you, and is constantly threatening to go out for competitive bids. Which customer is more valuable to you in the long run? The answer isn't always as clear-cut as one might think. Going through this LTV thought process can be helpful.

In sum, the customer is not always right, and a company needs to be comfortable and confident enough to tell them so when appropriate. Keeping customers happy is vital—but within reason. If your company always has to lose so the customer always wins—that's not a recipe for long-term mutual success. All customers are important, but not all customers are worth keeping. In fact, some customers should be fired. How you go about firing them is the key. A burned bridge creates a lot of smoke that others (customers, prospects, and competitors) will see; and it takes a long time to rebuild. Some customers should be fired, but done so with care.

The rest are customers you want to keep. They are all important, but that doesn't mean they are all equally important.

Fact: 20 percent of your customers account for 150 percent of your economic profit.

Fact: The bottom 20 percent of your customer base can generate losses equal to 150 percent of your profits.

Source: Larry Selden and Geoffrey Colvin, *Angel Customers & Demon Customers* (New York: Penguin, 2003), 56.

Customer Segmentation Is Vital

You'll recall our discussion in Chapter 1, where we said a company can't afford to tackle all the strategic goals it wants to at a given point in time. Similarly, you can't take, and shouldn't want to take, all customers to Level III relationships and profitability at a given point in time. This is where segmentation becomes increasingly important. It helps direct your attention, investment, and energy (your customer focus) to the segments with the most potential and achievable gain.

Organizations use many different methods and classifications to segment their customer base, and some industries have a generally accepted system for doing so. Typically, we see companies segmenting their customer base using one or more of the following common criteria:

- Industry segments (automotive, construction, aerospace, etc.)
- Geographical segments (states, districts, countries, regions, etc.)
- Channel segments (retail stores, online sales, catalogue sales, distributors, etc.)
- Product segments (different product lines or lines of service)
- Application segments (commercial, industrial, residential, municipal, etc.)

Some companies segment their customer base in terms of the sales process or, more specifically, what it takes to acquire, further penetrate, and retain a customer account. There are a wide range of criteria and labels we've seen used, but below are just a sampling of ideas:

- Sales Cycle (long, medium, or short lead time)
- Decision Maker (procurement department, technical buyer, general manager, etc.)
- Purchase Driver (price, convenience, value, brand preference, etc.)

- Competitors (numerous and effective, few but effective, few and ineffective, etc.)

In addition to those more common segmentation criteria, we also like companies to think further about their customer base in terms of the value involved:

- Value customers receive *from you* (what they need, expect, want, pay, and buy)
- Value they generate *for you* (sales, referrals, brand advocacy, margin growth, and LTV)
- Effort you expend to give and get that value (sales cycle, fulfillment and service cycle, and related costs)

10-Point Customer Focus Framework

#2. Customer Segmentation

The way a company chooses to segment its customer base using any of the above examples can vary widely. And, as you have probably surmised, there are benefits to all of them. The chief consideration here is: to which customers do you really want to devote your customer focus? Which ones represent the most potential of untapped value to you, and, with which ones do you have the best chance of successfully reaping that value? The following is a Segment-Priority Tool we often use to help a company segment and prioritize its customers for the specific purpose of determining whether they are a Level I, Level II, or Level III customer and which customers the company wants to advance within a particular level or from one level to the next.

This particular version of the tool uses six different segment characteristics (products, brand, referrals, share of wallet [SOW], potential, and relationship) to define each customer, and three different levels (A, B, and C) to evaluate each customer on each

SEGMENT CHARACTERISTICS & LEVELS			CUSTOMERS					
A	B	C	1	2	3	4	5	Etc.
PRODUCTS Bundle	Multiple	Single	A	C	B	B	A	–
BRAND Champion	Conservative	Critic	B	B	A	B	A	–
REFERRALS Many	Some	None	B	A	A	C	A	–
SOW Significant	Moderate	Limited	A	C	B	C	B	–
POTENTIAL Significant	Moderate	Limited	B	C	A	C	B	–
RELATIONSHIP Collaborative	Cooperative	Contentious	C	B	B	C	A	–
Customer Totals			36	23	45	14	50	–

Figure 3.1   Segment Evaluation Tool for Prioritizing Your Customer Base

characteristic. (See Figure 3.1.) Some companies actually apply different weights to the various characteristics to reflect different levels of importance to them. While the number, definitions, and weights, if applicable, of the characteristics and levels will vary widely based on the nature and goals of a particular company, here are the definitions for the specific version we illustrate in Figure 3.1:

Products—represents how much of your product or service portfolio is currently being purchased by a given customer. *Portfolio* refers to the full or complete array of products or services you offer. Each level (A, B, or C) can be further defined as a specific number of products or services, or as a percent of your total products or services.

Brand—represents the degree to which a customer prefers or actively promotes your brand over others. Some companies conduct regular market research or brand surveys to assess this and have formal metrics around it. Others may not. Again, the specific definitions of each level depend on the unique nature and goals or needs of the company.

Referrals—represent the number of times or frequency with which a customer takes a visible step to refer another prospective customer to you. Some companies have very specific criteria that define what steps, actions, or outcomes get credited as a referral.

SOW—commonly stands for *share of wallet*. Others call it *percent of customer spend*. In effect, it shows how much you're getting of a customer's total spend on certain products or services. For example, if a customer buys 10,000 widgets at $5,000 each, their total "widget spend" is $50,000,000. If they buy 3,600 of those widgets from you at $4,600 each, your share of their total wallet (or widget spend) is 36 percent (if in units) or roughly 33 percent (if in dollars).

Potential—represents the degree to which a company believes a customer will continue, or increase, their buying from the company in the future. Many companies do not have a good feel for this, but a fair number of companies use purchase history and buying patterns along with forecasting, predictive analytics, and modeling tools to try to define, quantify, and predict the purchase potential or LTV of a customer.

Relationship—refers to how easy it is to do business with a customer. Most companies rely on anecdotal information to evaluate customers in this characteristic. Some companies actually conduct internal surveys that gauge and capture perceptions and insights about how customers treat and deal with company employees in such areas as documenting sales terms and contracting, order entry and fulfillment, billing and A/R, and customer service and tech support, among others.

With those definitions in mind, this tool can then be used to evaluate and prioritize the various customers in a particular segment or in general. In this example, each customer (1, 2, 3, 4, 5, etc.) would get an A, B, or C rating for each of the six characteristics. Then using a formula where A = 10, B = 5, and C = 1, each customer gets a total score that ranges between 6 and 60.

Applying a scale we often use, any customer with an overall evaluation score over 50 is considered a low-risk customer with whom you're probably already enjoying a relationship somewhere between Level II and Level III of the Customer Focus Maturity Model® (CFMM). There's still significant progress to be made with them, but clearly no burning platform to address. Any customer with an overall evaluation score of less than 30 is considered an at-risk customer (retention, margin, penetration, or brand risks) and would be a viable candidate to start with or intensify a Level I focus.

But the real economic gain for you, generally speaking, will most likely come from focusing sharply on the middle group of customers—those with an overall evaluation score between 30 and 50. These are the customers who would value most from increasing your focus on them from Level I to Level II, or moving deeper into a Level II focus with them, or transitioning them from a Level II to a Level III focus. Accordingly, as they receive more value from your increasing focus, you're going to receive more value from their loyalty to you as a result. That is the heart of what the CFMM is all about. The ultimate goal is a loyalty relationship that improves to increasing and more sustained levels of mutual value or profitability. Let's look a bit more closely at this notion of loyalty.

Loyalty Generates Mutual Profitability

The ultimate goal of our customer focus journey is to get a company to the point where they are enjoying the mutual profitability that comes from a Level III relationship with their selected customers. That profitability is only possible when the customer–supplier relationship is characterized by a real sense of loyalty to each other. We'll define and refine what loyalty means to both sides more specifically as we proceed, but for now just think of it as being the optimal alignment of your customer's view of value, your brand promise, and your capability to deliver that customer's value and your promise, as shown in Figure 3.2.

Getting your customers to a point of loyalty requires first that you understand clearly what they value. As we discussed earlier, that value differs from one customer segment to the next. It can vary from one customer to the next within a given segment, and it will vary from one touch point to the next touch point within a given customer's organization. In addition, your customers' view of value can change

Figure 3.2   Loyalty Is the Target—Profit Is the Prize

just as their respective markets and customer needs will change. So, customer value is a multifaceted, dynamic target—continually evolving and morphing.

Next, you have to clearly pledge or declare your commitment to providing that value to them. Your brand promise must answer their value need and do so in a way that makes them come to you instead of going to a competitor for that value. It must answer these questions: *Why must I buy this value from you when there are other suppliers around who can also give me what I need? What makes you so different, and your value better than theirs?*

Finally, you have to make good on your pledge and deliver that value just as you said you would—just the way they requested it. That brand promise must be the common thread that connects your marketing and sales capabilities or activities to your design and production activities and in turn connects them to your fulfillment, distribution, billing, and service activities. You must have the capabilities within and throughout your company that enable you to make that promise real. In effect, that brand promise must pervade every aspect, every process, position, and person, every system, skill set, policy, and procedure—literally, every nook and cranny of your

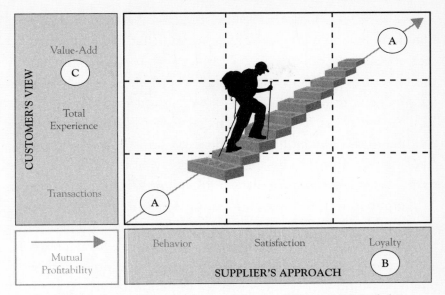

Figure 3.3 The Customer Focus Maturity Model

organization. It must be a shaper and core driver of your company's culture. Ultimately, it must be your company's culture!

We hope you're beginning to form a much clearer picture of the close linkage that exists between your customer focus (loyalty) and your business goals (profitability). That linkage is there whether you choose to recognize and leverage it or you choose to ignore it. If you ignore it, the disconnect between your strategy and customer focus will forever be a speed bump to your growth and success. If you chose to recognize and leverage it, you're in for a great ride.

Mutual Profitability Starts the Customer Focus Journey

Let's introduce and start building the Customer Focus Maturity Model® by recapping some of our key discussion points thus far. (See Figure 3.3.) First, realize that you're in business to make money by creating and delivering value to your customers. Your goal is a win–win relationship or mutual profitability (A).

As a supplier, you further realize that customer behavior and satisfaction are only part of the picture and that the real gains you seek come from your customers' loyalty (B). You build that loyalty by delivering customers value that goes beyond the transaction and adds value at every touch point of the customers' total experience (C). Any number of suppliers can give your customers the value they get in the standard business deal or transaction. The competitive differentiator is to be able to identify what is important to the customers beyond that standard transaction. What do they view as a differentiator at each touch point of the entire customer experience, and how can you turn each touch point into an opportunity to deliver added value (beyond what your competitors can provide) consistently, over time? Just as important, how can you turn each touch point into a barrier to entry for any competitor?

CHAPTER

4

When Customers Speak— Who Hears Them?

- Voice of the customer (VOC)—pros and cons
- Top 10 reasons customers leave
- Listening to voices beyond the transaction

Almost all new customer–supplier relationships begin with a transaction where the customer behaves in one way and the supplier behaves in a certain way as a result of it (or vice versa). The customer pays the supplier and the supplier provides a product or service. Some suppliers are content with that transaction model. Many are not. They know that a competitor's cheaper, faster transaction is waiting around every corner. For those suppliers, the challenge becomes: *How do you keep this customer's transactions with you and keep your competitors out of the picture? How do you keep your customers satisfied enough to stay with you?* This is the point where many companies start their customer focus. This is Level I of the Customer Focus Maturity Model® (CFMM)—a very basic level,

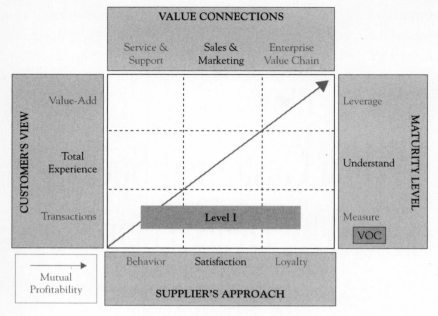

Figure 4.1   Level I of the CFMM

but a very important foundational level that must be managed well before progressing to higher levels. (See Figure 4.1.)

Level I—Voice of the Customer (VOC)

Most companies at Level I start their customer focus journey because they have experienced some type of customer risk such as rising customer complaints, increased turnover, unusual pricing pressure, lower contract renewal rates, and so forth. Some companies, though the minority based on our experience, start their Level I efforts as a preventative maintenance initiative as a new competitor, new customer, or new market enters the scene and although the company has no currently known problems or risks, they don't want to be surprised and caught unprepared.

Level I companies most often begin their customer focus efforts with some type of process or program to assess the voice of the customer (VOC). VOC activities include a wide range of steps or processes a company takes or applies to enable, solicit, encourage, and use customer input. The most common benefit a company seeks from a VOC effort is to uncover instances and causes of any customer dissatisfaction, complaints, defections, or other problems. In essence, VOC efforts help to detect the customers' unmet needs. There are a number of different techniques companies use to discover such problems. We'll briefly describe some of the more prevalent ones:

- Customer surveys
- Customer focus groups
- Customer interviews
- On-site assessments
- Customer communities

In general, we see companies use three different types of survey processes—*periodic surveys, transactional surveys,* or *incident-based surveys*. Periodic surveys are typically conducted on some preset schedule, such as quarterly, semiannually, annually, or biannually. They are conducted for a large portion, or all, of a company's customer base on a certain recurring schedule, and are often supplemented by smaller-scale interim surveys of a cross-section sample of the customer base or a particular customer segment. The periodic surveys we see most often used are ones based on satisfaction, loyalty, or net promoter metrics.

Transactional surveys are usually conducted after select types of transactions or touch points. For example, signing a sales contract, placing an online or phone order, arranging for credit or financing, placing a customer support or service call or inquiry, and having a product serviced, repaired, or exchanged are all examples of transactions that might trigger a survey from the supplier.

Some companies use incident-based surveys that are typically administered after a complaint has been filed or a customer has encountered some type of problem. One thing a surprising number of companies don't do, however, is send an incident survey to a customer who has defected. Too many companies are reluctant to take this important step and the reasons we most often hear are: they'd rather not further aggravate the customer by asking for input after the fact; they don't want to appear desperate for business or admitting to mistake; and they just don't have a good mechanism or control in place to follow-up in an effective and consistent way. This is a huge missed opportunity. Granted there are some defecting customers who will be further aggravated by it, and some who might view it as a sign of weakness or guilt. But hey—they've already taken their business elsewhere. What more harm can they do to you? The fact is, not much—if it's handled appropriately.

There are valuable insights to be learned and possibly something to be gained from following up with customers who defect. At a minimum, it's important to get their view as to why they left, which won't necessarily match the reasons they give your sales or customer support personnel. The ten reasons—other than or in addition to price—we most often hear customers tell us they leave a particular supplier, in no particular order, are:

- Poor handling of a complaint—even a single incident.
- Unexplained changes in policy, price, product, or sales force.
- Customer misinterpretation or mistake.
- Supplier employees are disingenuous, abrasive, or don't consistently apply policies.
- Products or services don't meet requested or promised expectations.
- Promises are made but not kept; poor follow-up or follow-through.
- Late, inaccurate, or terse communications from supplier.
- Customer expectations were unrealistic or not managed well by supplier.
- Poor quality of delivery, installation, or post-sale service.
- Customer felt taken for granted; customer felt treated like a transaction.

Clearly, the supplier who's reluctant to follow-up with a defecting customer will often go on thinking it was due solely to price, and will miss the opportunity to possibly improve some internal process, policy, or capability. Moreover, they'll miss the opportunity to engage the unhappy customer one more time and possibly reopen the door that had been slammed shut. Incident-based surveys and related recovery efforts can be an effective tool for existing, as well as defecting, customers.

Some people view transactional and incident-based surveys as one and the same, but the incident-based survey is usually a damage-control step whereas a transactional survey may or may not be in response to a problem or risk, and may be just as preventative as it is remedial.

Customer focus groups can be an effective means of gaining in-depth insights from customers, whether the customers are of similar or mixed characteristics, and they can be an effective way to road-test upcoming key initiatives, new offerings, or change in a company's process. Customer focus groups can be difficult or time consuming to coordinate, as it usually takes some effort to persuade enough customers to participate. They also require a certain skill to effectively facilitate.

Customer interviews are excellent, but underused, vehicles for gaining some of the additional insights or addressing some of the nuances mentioned above about surveys and focus groups. The key drawbacks about interviews is that they take a certain amount of courage to face a customer one-on-one, and they take a lot of effort to cover enough customers to obtain any macro or market-wide insights. They are, however, excellent for probing deeply into the views and needs of specific customers.

For example, Wachovia is said to use a third-party organization to conduct customer interviews after various touch point experiences, with at least 300,000 interviews being conducted in a year's time. But you don't need to be big, or use external resources, to benefit from these steps. Stoner Inc., a small (about 50 employees) specialty manufacturer of cleaning, lubrication, and coating products, is a great example. Stoner supplements its formal customer survey process with a structured approach to contacting current, prospective, and former customers each week to hold more personal and productive dialogues with them. More than 1,000 customer contacts are made each week by the Stoner team.[1]

On-site assessments are a tool that many organizations don't know or think about and consequently don't use as much as they could or should. In essence, an on-site assessment is a type of audit that targets specific touch points of the customer–supplier relationship. It typically uses brief, structured questionnaires and/or interviews conducted by the supplier company's personnel. Each questionnaire or interview is tailored to the specific processes, tasks, or activities involved at that particular touch point. Oftentimes the supplier company will dispatch a small team that coordinates the assessment participants and timing with the customer such that the team is in and out in a half-day's time or less.

These assessments can produce the depth of insights comparable to those gleaned from interviews, but they have the added advantage of targeting different aspects of the overall customer–supplier relationship. So they provide the depth of an interview in a much more comprehensive picture. They do have drawbacks, however, being time consuming and more intrusive than surveys and requiring much more design time than focus groups or interviews.

Lastly, customer communities can be important sources of customer insights. They can reflect the sentiments—both favorable and critical—from a broad range and large number of customers but cannot be readily managed or controlled. Experience shows that it is best for a company to create and openly encourage such communities rather than wait for your customer base to do it for you in a less structured, non–company-sponsored venue. Usually, when customers form communities themselves, they originate, and possibly never get away from, negative insights. If the community is moderated or managed to some extent by the sponsoring company, it does provide the company with a forum to respond to and possibly correct any problems or perceptions.

---

[1] Kristen Johnson, "Stoner: Built on a Strong Foundation," *Quality Progress* (August 2004): 40.

One of the most well-known and effective customer communities may be the Harley Owners Group (H.O.G.) that Harley-Davidson spawned many years ago. H.O.G. has become an institution that over the years has drawn customers from all walks of life—from boardwalks to boardrooms. H.O.G. members come together to share, promote, and support their Harley experience though biker rallies, H.O.G. clubs, clothing, accessories, and the like, all of which have shaped a group of brand advocates that is clearly unique and pervasive.

The above discussion about VOC tools is meant to be illustrative, not comprehensive. Clearly, there are others we haven't mentioned. There are also ways of combining the features and benefits of one tool with another to create hybrids, and there are other pros and cons of these specific tools. In general, these and other VOC techniques can be very effective at enabling, soliciting, encouraging, and gathering customer input. Three key points must be kept in mind for any company at Level I.

1. The best VOC processes use a combination of more than one technique or tool.
2. The best VOC processes, especially surveys, engage customers in their design.
3. Customer input is useless, and actually risky, if you don't do something with it.

The first point above is self-explanatory. Different approaches work better or worse for different segments and different customers at different times and under different circumstances. Customer focus never has been, and never will be, a one-size-fits-all solution.

The second point was already illustrated in Chapter 2, when we talked about using metrics that matter the most (i.e., metrics that matter to the customer). Despite how obvious it seems to engage the customer beforehand, many companies don't. Most just don't think about doing it, some fear doing it, and a significant number don't know how to do it.

The third point warrants further attention. Whether you engage them beforehand or not, customers are generally going to be more than willing to respond to their supplier's survey—especially if it's the supplier's first survey attempt. Most customers view surveys as meaningful tools as long as they believe the supplier is actually listening to and doing something with the feedback. It's a shame to see how many suppliers conduct surveys and then do a poor job of planning and managing post-survey follow-up and communications. Worse is the number of companies that conduct a survey, do little or no meaningful follow-up, and then expect customers to react well the next time the supplier sends a subsequent survey.

A survey is like other customer–supplier transactions in many respects—one being that it requires follow-up and management of expectations. Companies must have a plan for managing the results. That plan should answer each of the questions in the list below (and there may be others your company could add). Each answer should be followed by the most important management question of all: *Who will do what by when and with whom?*

- How are you going to analyze the data or responses?
- How are you going to prioritize the identified issues?
- What are the potential follow-up actions, and what specifically does that follow-up look like?
- How will you ensure that a follow-up action does, in fact, happen?
- How will you manage any unique customer issues that need to be addressed?
- How will you identify and handle any programmatic or system-wide issues revealed?
- How will you circle back to all participating and nonparticipating customers?
- How will you improve future survey efforts as a result of what you learned?

Many of these same follow-up steps apply to any number of VOC activities—not just surveys. Anything you do to solicit customer input must have a corresponding plan for using or responding to that input. Customers will usually give you credit just for taking a step to understand their perceptions, measure their satisfaction, or otherwise solicit their input. But they want to know that your interest was sincere, that their input was reviewed, and that something will happen as a result of it. Until you've proved that to them, it's best that you don't even think about surveying them again.

Advantages and Limitations of VOC

To summarize, voice of the customer techniques are generally quite effective for a company relatively new to Level I, or for a company struggling with defining its Level I approach. There are some clear and consistent benefits of VOC efforts, including the following.

Benefits of VOC Efforts

- Can cover a large population of customers with a single effort.
- Can be time efficient and minimally disruptive to the customer.
- Most activities are easy to self-administer.
- The supplier typically "gets credit" just for asking.
- Can be very effective at detecting problems that may have gone unreported.
- Creates expectations that can motivate and align supplier personnel.
- The supplier typically "gets more credit" for addressing a detected problem.
- Many VOC tools can be used to quantify (measure) risks and progress.
- Can effectively surface the customer's unmet needs.

Two of those benefits are particularly compelling. One is the credit a typical customer gives you for fixing a problem. According to J. D. Powers, "data shows that customer encounters in which a problem is resolved quickly and efficiently receive higher satisfaction scores than situations in which there was no problem at all."[2] When there are issues, they tend to appreciate and value the interest, humbleness, and responsiveness of their suppliers—within reason. In sum, Level I efforts are particularly effective for recovery situations. The second key benefit is the ability to measure progress. Being able to quantify, track, monitor, evaluate, improve, and reward progress is critical to the execution of any business initiative. Similarly, it becomes increasingly vital to a company's customer focus efforts, as we'll be describing in more detail when we discuss Level III.

There are also several important limitations of VOC activities to consider. Some of these we've already mentioned, but we present them below in one list.

- Too many VOC efforts are based solely on the supplier's view of what's important.
- A significant number of the related tools are poorly designed.
- Communications before, during, and after the VOC process or activity must be effective.
- Many VOC activities are viewed as being "owned" by the customer service, customer care, or customer support teams.
- Most efforts engage a slice of the customer base and experience that's too narrow.
- A number of VOC actions are limited to the point of sale or closely related functions.

These last two points are particularly noteworthy. By their very nature, voice-of-the-customer tools ask customers about their

---

[2] Chris Denove and James D. Power IV, *Satisfaction: How Every Great Company Listens to the Voice of the Customer* (New York: Penguin, 2006), 182.

experiences with you—their current supplier. In many cases, however, a customer's expectations of a supplier may actually have been shaped by the customer's experience with a supplier in another, different industry. Typical VOC tools and techniques cannot effectively get to the levels and types of discussions that will reveal those "perceptions from the periphery."

In addition to this nuance, the customer organization is a multifaceted, multilayered entity. The "customer experience" for such an organization goes far beyond the sales transaction and the buyer-and-seller players involved in that transaction. There are numerous other people in the customer organization who interact with the supplier's product, service, people, systems, and processes. These include technical advisors and influencers who collaborate with the procurement staff. There are operations people and end users as well as service and maintenance personnel who might have to use or support use of the supplier's product or service. There are executive sponsors and other management players who must informally endorse or formally approve the purchase decision. And there are accounting and claims personnel, shipping and receiving employees, receptionists and admin support staff, among others—all of whom have some type of "experience" with the supplier.

Similarly, there are myriad other people in the supplier organization who interact with the customer's people, systems, and processes—even with the customer's products in some cases.

Every player in the customer organization is an important touch point or part of the entire customer–supplier relationship. Every one of them has their own view of what it means to be "easy to do business with." Every one of them has their own respective expectations, pain points, and definitions of value. Any one of them can influence their company's decision to continue doing business with (or do more business or less business with) a respective supplier. Any one of them might have a voice someone in the customer organization is going to listen to and be influenced by. Unfortunately, most supplier VOC activities only focus on one or two key players in the customer

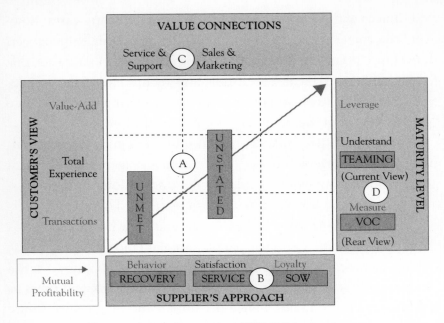

Figure 4.2   Assessing VOC Limitations

organization. They only hear one or two of the voices, and miss the others—the voices of others who might be talking about them.

So you, as the supplier company, need some way to hear as many of those voices as possible. You need connections that go beyond the initial buy decision or sale transaction. The more connections the supplier has in the customer organization, and the deeper into the customer organization those connections go, the more a supplier can learn about the customers—what they need, and exactly how they need it to be provided. Thus, the harder it will be for a competitor to pry that customer away. It's a lot harder to break the grip of multiple relationships than it is to break the grip of one.

There are a few other limitations of Level I efforts or activities that suppliers must understand. (See Figure 4.2, which illustrates the points A, B, C, and D in the following discussion.)

A. Typical VOC efforts can be effective at identifying the needs or concerns of a customer that are not being met, but they aren't effective at flushing out a customer's unstated needs—the needs they won't share with a traditional transaction supplier, and needs they won't share with a supplier unless their relationship is one of proven trust, confidence, and cooperation (i.e., a relationship in which the supplier has demonstrated a track record of "getting it right"). You need a way of mining the pieces of information to reveal the customer's unstated needs.

B. In uncovering the unmet needs, VOC can be effective at helping the supplier recover from a mistake or service misstep. If acted on quickly enough, it can even help identify and prevent a customer defection. VOC efforts can also help identify ideas and ways to further improve customer service and satisfaction. However, they are not sufficient for flushing out ways to increase your share of the customer's wallet (SOW) or spend.

C. Because VOC activities are usually assigned to or owned by a supplier's customer service or customer support functions, other key stakeholders and connections in the supplier organization don't own the process and thus don't always support or optimize their role in it. To understand the customer's complete need for value and their view of the total experience, many others in the supplier organization must engage the customer in uniquely effective ways.

D. Most VOC activities measure or gauge the status of the relationship at a specific point in time. Moreover, VOC activities look at things that have already happened—a look in the rearview mirror. So VOC is more of a snapshot than an ongoing feed of insights, and it's outdated by the time you learn about it. Suppliers need a more dynamic (evolving) and a more current (real-time) understanding of their customers.

Level II of the CFMM is the "teaming level," which addresses the above limitations and moves the customer focus journey to the next phase of effectiveness and profitability. The teaming we'll describe is not the type of teamwork most people think of when they first hear the term. At this level, we'll describe unique and very effective ways of working across the customer–supplier boundary with the following purpose or objectives:

- Engaging customers in a way that uncovers their unstated needs—needs that can put the supplier company at a unique competitive advantage—and ways to stay abreast of those real-time needs as they evolve.

- Developing a deeper and more comprehensive view of what value means to the broader customer organization and using that understanding to provide increasingly more value to them, gaining more of their business and creating more barriers to entry for your competitors.

- Identify ways of equipping and engaging a broader range of supplier personnel in ways that create a greater number of—and longer-term—mutually beneficial customer–supplier relationships. Level II multiplies the number of people who are actively thinking about and looking for ways to further differentiate your organization.

In Chapter 5 we present Level II of the customer focus journey.

Customers consistently and emphatically tell us: The cost of doing business with a supplier goes far beyond the sale.

Input Is Vital—But Involvement Multiplies the Value

- Move from points of parity, to differentiation, to unique value propositions
- Level II Teaming—turning touch points into sources of value
- Customer engagement techniques that work

Many companies stay at Level I for several years, and others never progress. That fact itself isn't necessarily bad. If a supplier company has a solid mechanism in place to reveal, effectively resolve, and recover from customer complaints and concerns, that may be sufficient for them. This is especially true if they are not experiencing problematic turnover, losing an unacceptable number of new customer bids or proposals, and are happy with the customer's share of wallet they have. We realize that a Level II customer focus isn't for everyone. You may not feel you need it. Here are some of the more common symptoms that tell a company they could benefit from taking their focus to this next level:

- The same or similar types of customer problems, issues, or complaints tend to recur.
- You have a hard time building cost increases into your pricing structure.
- Certain customer needs can't be clearly identified or consistently met.
- Your company isn't happy with the number, size, or type of customers who are defecting.
- Problems get resolved with one customer only to surface with some other customer.
- You're losing more bids, proposals, or tenders than you want to lose.
- Your customer focus results are good in one part of the business but not in another.
- You want to increase your share of your customer's wallet.
- Your customer economics are good in some segments but not in others.
- You need to improve the market uptake of new products or services.
- Too many of your customers seem to make decisions based solely on price.
- You want to accelerate your penetration of accounts with additional products or services.
- You can't convincingly differentiate your products or services from those of your competitors.
- You want to create more barriers to entry with your key customers.

If one or more of the above factors apply to your company, then you could benefit from a deeper or more comprehensive focus on your customers. Please note that oftentimes the rigor and opportunities associated with Level II efforts result in the need for fundamental changes in processes, organizational structures or roles, or people (capabilities and skills). That level of change can represent formidable challenges for some companies. But Level II can significantly help a company make more than the incremental gains or short-term improvements typical of Level I, and it can move them much further along the profit curve of the Customer Focus Maturity Model (CFMM).

Differentiation—One Touch Point at a Time

The key to the activities and objectives of a Level II customer focus is to know what it takes to consistently differentiate your company, and the customer's experience with your company, from that of your competitors. As we've already mentioned, that differentiation must come in the form of value that you provide that your competitors cannot provide. Let's begin by generally understanding three concepts from the customer's perspective (see Figure 5.1) that are a core part of the differentiated value suppliers must identify and provide.

A. Points of parity (POPs) are attributes or benefits your company provides that usually are not unique to you and are shared by any number of your competitors. POPs are the minimum requirements to be in the game, and most suppliers strive to at least match their competitor's claimed attributes or benefits—just to play in a particular market. Since most competitors have or claim to have these attributes, they usually are not the reason a customer will choose one brand (supplier) over another. A supplier that lacks certain POP will likely not be considered a credible player in that market and will usually not be invited to compete (bid) by the customer.

B. Points of differentiation (PODs) are attributes or benefits customers consistently associate with a particular brand or supplier,

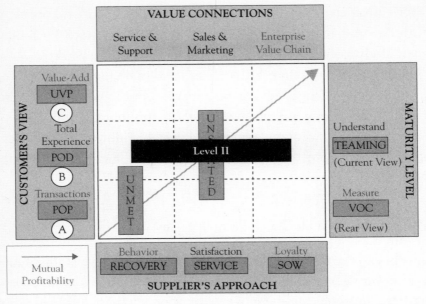

Figure 5.1   Customer Focus Maturity Model®

and view as favorable attributes they could not find to the same degree at most, if not all, of your competitors. PODs are attributes with which a company claims superiority over their competitors, or exclusiveness over similar products or services offered by competitors. In our experience, most companies are overly confident about the number of PODs they realistically have, and they are generally uninformed about the PODs their competitors have or claim to have.

C. Unique value proposition (UVP) is the supplier's promise or commitment to deliver, for a price (i.e., the proposition aspect), a specific value that other competing suppliers cannot or do not provide (POD). The product or service provided is uniquely valuable to that particular customer in that it fulfills their need for a specific gain, benefit, or advantage. The UVP is the promise a supplier describes in such a way that lets the customer know: *Here's the important benefit or value your company gets from us that you specifically need or want, and that only we can give to you.*

POP—minimum value required by this market—all suppliers can provide it and so can we.

POD—unique value that only our company can provide—it's our differentiation.

UVP—unique value that only we provide and here's how that benefits you, our customer.

With this basic understanding, remember that "value" is in the eyes of the beholder and it can differ from segment to segment, customer to customer, and person to person within a customer company. So the objective at Level II is to explore, define, test, improve, and leverage the unique value proposition the supplier can deliver at each touch point in the customer–supplier relationship. You might not be able to identify a clear unique value proposition for every touch point. For some you might only be able to identify a differentiator. The key is to never settle for a touch point that represents parity for your company, because that touch point can become an entry point for a competitor.

(See the sidebar, *Experience the Touch Points of Tech Box Company*, which describes a typical customer scenario.)

Each touch point represents an "anticipate moment." And every moment or point of interaction is an opportunity to block the competition . . . or let it in.

By now, you might realize this is not an overnight process. It can take a supplier some time to discover or define a unique way to serve, support, or engage a particular touch point. But the fact is that while you're working at it, you're learning more and more about the customer at that touch point, and they're becoming more and more convinced of your genuine interest in them. Underneath all of that effort, a solid working relationship and a deeper con-nection is developing. There's nothing wrong with that—right? Remember, we call this a journey, not an event. It's a marathon, not a sprint. If you think you're going to try a couple of quick tech-niques, chalk up a couple touch-point wins, and expect to have a competitive advantage—think again.

To recap, the overarching objective of Level II is to:

- Develop a deep understanding of how customers define value at the various touch points in their company

- Add value throughout your customers' entire experience with your company

- Do that in such a unique way or with such unique value that customers are increasingly loyal to you and that loyalty trans-lates into barriers to entry and mutual profitability

Experience the Touch Points of Tech Box Company

Here's a scenario that most of us have undoubtedly experi-enced as either a homeowner or renter. Walk in the shoes of this customer, Mr. Jones, and see how Tech Box Company managed and leveraged the various touch points of his cus-tomer experience.

Background

This scenario involves a regional company that markets, dis-tributes, installs, and services high-end electrical home appli-ances for a five-state area. We'll refer to them as the supplier in this illustration and call them Tech Box Company (TBC). They aren't the only supplier in the region that markets, dis-tributes, and installs these particular products. But they are one of the few, and the largest one, in the area that provides in-home service. Let's assume you are the customer, Mr. Jones, and you bought one of their appliances two months ago (in June). The appliance needs to be serviced. So you call their 24/7 toll-free number to schedule an in-home service call. The process that call goes through has three primary touch points:

1. The initial customer inquiry on the 800 line
2. The scheduling of the service visit
3. The actual in-home service visit

The Initial Service Call

Your initial inquiry call goes in to a customer care associate who promptly and very professionally answers the phone, is very quick but polite in getting to the heart of your need, and graciously offers to connect you to a field service coordinator. The customer care associate makes the phone line connection, refers to the field service coordinator by his or her first name (and to you by your formal name), and makes a first-class introduction. "Hello, Keith, this is Mary in customer care and I have on the line with me Mr. Jones (that's you, the customer), who would like to schedule an in-home service call. Do you have a moment to help Mr. Jones?" Keith promptly responds, "Absolutely, Mary, I'd be delighted to. Good morning, Mr. Jones. I see Mary has already keyed in your information, so I think I have everything I need. Is this service call for the same address where we installed the appliance in June?" A bit surprised by their efficient and responsive process, you answer, "Yes it is."

Then you hear Keith striking his computer keys while he explains he's looking for the next available technical service advisor who can visit your home. After just a few seconds, he says, "We at TBC really appreciate your business, Mr. Jones, and I personally really appreciate your patience here this morning. It looks like we can get that visit scheduled

(continued)

for you on Thursday the 12th. Would morning or afternoon be better for you?" You unhappily realize that's three days away, but they are just about the only credible service provider in town, and they have given you a first-rate customer experience on this call. You pause, and finally say, "Afternoon," with a hint of disappointment in your voice. Keith, obviously picking up on your disappointment, says, "I know that's a couple days away, Mr. Jones, so do you have a preference for the time? Our technical service advisor can be there between noon and 2:00, between 2:00 and 4:00, or between 4:00 and 6:00 that afternoon—whichever one works better for you."

You're a little bit, though not very, impressed that they're acting like you have a choice, and you admit that it does provide you with some flexibility—assuming they actually show up during the window you choose. So you say, "2:00 to 4:00." He replies, "Perfect. I have you down for 2:00 this Thursday. Your technical service advisor will be Josh. If Josh can get there earlier, he'll call you first to see if that works for you. If Josh does not arrive in time to complete your service by 4:00, the service call will be free. Let me quickly confirm that address once more, and the number Josh can call you on that day." You confirm the information for him, and he closes with, "Thank you once again for your business, Mr. Jones. We appreciate the chance to serve you. Again, my name is Keith, and I hope you won't hesitate to call on us if you need anything else. And please enjoy the rest of your Monday, sir."

The Service Visit

Thursday comes around, and not a minute too soon in your view. At 1:45, you get a call from Josh, your technical service advisor, who says he's finishing up a job on the other side of town, and will be to your house by 3:30. He arrives at 3:25. Dressed in a TBC uniform, well groomed and personable, Josh greets you and confirms that it's still a convenient time to service your appliance. You lead him to the room where the appliance is located, and he speedily gets to work. As he begins taking off the cover panel, he asks you a couple of questions. He wants you to describe what the problem was, when you first experienced it, did it happen every time or intermittently, and how long did it last each time. He continues working quickly and diligently as you answer his questions. You describe the problem and explain that it started a week ago, was intermittent at first, but for the past three days has been doing it every time. It starts as soon as you turn the unit on, and it lasts until you turn the unit off. You have not been able to get the unit to operate at all for the past three days, despite numerous attempts each day.

After about 15 minutes, Josh excuses himself to go to his truck for a moment. You decide to make a quick phone call while he's away. He returns after two or three minutes, and seeing you are on the phone, without pause goes directly back to working on your appliance. He finishes his repair, reassembles the disconnected parts, and turns the unit back on. Success! Giving you a thumbs-up sign, he whispers, "That should do it. I doubt you'll be having any more problems with it, but just call if you do." He leaves it running for a few minutes while he completes some paperwork. You are still on the phone, but with a sense of relief you interrupt your call to ask him if he needs a check, or will TBC send you a bill. He whispers, "No charge for the visit, Mr. Jones. It's our pleasure. I'll leave a copy of the completed service slip with you for your records. Will there be anything else before I leave?" You whisper back, "Nothing else right now, and thank you for handling this for me. I do appreciate it." It was now 4:00. And since you were still wrapping up your phone call, Josh smiled and politely let himself out. The unit ran fine for the rest of the day and has been running fine ever since.

(continued)

The Analysis

By most standards, and in most customers' views, this was a positive customer experience. Mr. Jones would probably give good ratings on any post-service call survey, and would probably respond positively to any other type of customer survey from TBC. More likely than not, he would also have favorable things to say about TBC to other people looking to buy such an appliance or in need of service. TBC clearly detected and met his unmet needs—an effective Level I focus.

However, TBC missed numerous opportunities to reap the gains of a Level II customer focus. As prompt, polite, and efficient as the customer care associate was, she was more focused on getting the customer connected to the next link in the process than she was optimizing her time with the customer. She could have briefly probed in any number of other areas that would have aided TBC in serving this customer even better, while deepening her personal connection with the customer. Questions such as:

Can you describe the problem or symptoms for me?

When was the first time you experienced it?

Does it happen all the time or only sporadically?

Have you tried anything to fix it or have you had anyone else look at it yet?

Have you had problems with this unit before now?

Other questions that might indicate the need for special parts, equipment, tools, or service advisor skills

The field service coordinator was mostly focused on determining when the next service technician could or would be in Mr. Jones's neighborhood or vicinity. Other considerations the coordinator could have focused on or asked about include:

For how long had the customer already been without service?

Had other service visits been scheduled but not performed?

Had other service visits been performed that weren't successful?

What could be learned from the previous service advisor who called on this customer?

Was there anything about the customer's home or location that would impact the truck being sent, or the need for more than one service person (for lifting or moving the appliance, for instance)?

Josh, the technical service advisor, was understandably focused on getting the repair done as quickly and correctly as possible. But, as TBC's only face-to-face touch point in this example, and actually being at the location where their appliance was in use, he had a unique opportunity, which he missed. Unfortunately, any dialogue he had with Mr. Jones was to get answers to questions that could have been asked earlier in the process—before he arrived. What if the fix wasn't as straightforward as it was in this case? What steps were taken to ensure Josh arrived with the right tools, the right parts, or the right knowledge about that particular product or model? What would have happened at 4:01 if Josh didn't have the unit fixed? Stay late? Leave, as he had another visit to make, and reschedule you for another day? Refer you back to the 800 number to get rescheduled? But even more importantly, Josh didn't take, or wasn't permitted to take, the time to advance TBC's reputation or deepen his relationship with Mr. Jones. He could have taken such steps as:

Explaining to Mr. Jones what he suspected the problem to be, or what the problem and solution ultimately were.

Educating Mr. Jones on any self-diagnosis or preventative maintenance.

(continued)

Understand how the appliance was being used and who in the house used it.

See if there were any other TBC products, or competitor products, in the house.

Make recommendations on other TBC products or services Mr. Jones might like.

Reinforce how well the appliance performed other than this "isolated" problem.

Verify and reinforce the fact that Mr. Jones was happy with the service call and visit.

Josh did just as he was expected to do at Level I. But he also had significant opportunity to identify additional revenue possibilities with Mr. Jones, gain competitive insights, promote brand loyalty, and possibly start building some barrier to competitive entry or repeat competitor business.

The entire service call process at TBC was efficient, effective, and professional—from beginning to end. It was a typical Level I transaction around a stated but unmet need. It was also a missed opportunity for gaining a Level II understanding of the customer's unstated needs, identifying ways to further differentiate TBC, and adding revenue opportunities. In essence, TBC missed the chance to convert their touch points into anticipate moments.

Teaming Turns Feedback into Dialogue

The processes and techniques we use to turn feedback into dialogue make up the core of the Level II customer focus. *Teaming* is the umbrella under which we group all of those processes and techniques.

Teaming requires deploying several more elements from the 10-Point Customer Focus Framework we introduced back in Chapter 1. So let's turn to some additional elements.

10-Point Customer Focus Framework

#3. Customer Engagement

The most common and natural step many companies take to progress to the insights of Level II is to first multiply the number of "listening posts" they use to solicit, gather, and respond to the voice of the customer (VOC). VOC is still a useful step in Level II, but only if it taps into more than the typical one or two customer touch points. Buyers and decision makers are only a part of the picture. Technical influencers, end-users, quality assurance (QA) and maintenance personnel, logistics, information technology (IT) and accounting staff, and myriad other customer representatives are all potential key touch points for which Level II suppliers want avenues to solicit, synthesize, and incorporate their input.

The other important step is to turn or extend your listening tools into dialogue vehicles. This entails using the VOC tools to probe more deeply into the perspectives, expectations, and needs of the customer representative at each touch point. To do that requires customizing these tools to the particular function or department involved in that touch point. This is difficult to do in survey tools without making them unduly cumbersome and time consuming for the customer respondent. The key is to use traditional VOC surveys to efficiently surface the key issues and general needs of the customer company, and set the stage for more in-depth, touch point–specific, follow-up dialogues to come later. That more in-depth, follow-up dialogue can be in the form of phone or face-to-face interviews, functional or departmental focus groups, or on-site assessments. We described on-site assessments back in Chapter 4, but we'll take a closer look now at interviews and focus groups—two effective dialogue techniques that help suppliers gain the deeper customer involvement we seek at Level II.

Touch point surveys and interviews are a key step for one particular organization with whom we work. They use a biannual survey tool that goes to several different members of each customer organization and addresses the same structured satisfaction and loyalty measures that the supplier uses for all customers being surveyed that year. Based on the issues or ideas generated in that biannual survey, several different functional or department-specific surveys (i.e., touch point surveys) are then sent to department representatives in each responding customer company. Those surveys are tailored to the specific activities, processes, or tasks unique to a given department, functional area, or touch point. They are designed to surface the issues and needs at each touch point that require more dialogue (i.e., an interview) to fully explain and understand. The intent is to get in front of the person representing that touch point for the customer and begin a dialogue that digs deeper into the individual's own personal views of what's working well and not so well; what's most important to him or her and what's not important. More specifically, that touch point interview is intended to begin flushing out what that individual views as examples of parity (POP), differentiation (POD), and unique value (UVP) in his or her respective role.

Another organization uses an annual satisfaction survey process with follow-up functional or departmental focus groups (i.e., touch point focus groups) to dig more deeply into the survey results for, and establish dialogues with, a targeted function, department, or process. For example, based on the annual survey results, the supplier company might see a cluster of issues or unmet needs that pertain to the supplier's order entry system. The supplier company will then organize a focus group consisting of functional or department-specific representatives from various customer companies who have to use the supplier's order entry system. The touch point focus group is used to probe further into the participants' personal views of what's working well and not so well; what's most important to them and what's not important—when it comes to placing and tracking orders with the supplier. More specifically, the supplier is looking for what the focus group participants view as points of parity, differentiation, or unique value in their respective roles, in their respective companies.

As noted earlier, because of the diverse companies, personalities, and possible issues represented in a focus group like this, care must be taken in the design and facilitation of these group discussions. They can be very effective at digging deeper and beginning the dialogue that turns into a longer lasting relationship, a source of value-creating insights, and a barrier to the competition.

As you can imagine, when suppliers multiply the number of their VOC listening posts beyond the initial sale, and use selected dialogue techniques to drill more deeply into the relationships at various touch points, they can reap several benefits:

- The chance to probe, ask, and answer questions that aren't possible with surveys.

- Invaluable insights into the customers' unmet (POP) and unstated (POD) needs.

- Understanding what's important to each individual customer that might be unique to them or to the suppliers' capabilities.

- The opportunity to establish a personal connection or relationship that goes beyond the sales transaction.

- The chance to maintain and gradually leverage that relationship into further competitive advantage over time.

And since each of the above benefits can be generated for multiple touch points, suppliers gain the advantage of developing a uniquely comprehensive view of their customers' value needs and opportunities. And the more they meet those needs and capitalize on those opportunities, the stronger the relationships become across the entire spectrum of customer–supplier connections, and the harder it will be for a competitor to break those various relationships or connections.

In addition to the above-mentioned VOC tools, there are several other dialogue techniques that can have a similar impact on establishing additional and deeper touch points—the kind that establish and leverage unique customer–supplier relationships. (See Figure 5.2.) These include customer advisory boards,

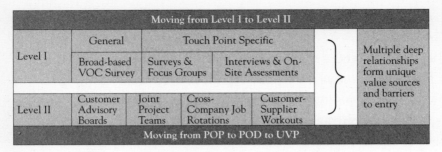

Figure 5.2   Transitioning from Techniques in Level I to Level II

joint project teams, job rotations and customer–supplier work-outs (to be discussed in Chapter 7), among others.

Customer advisory boards (CABs) provide an excellent example. A CAB is typically a group of customer representatives who are invited to serve as an advisory board to the supplier company. The CAB is made up of anywhere from 6 to 10 members (sometimes more, and sometimes less) who serve for a specified period of time (1–3 years seems to be the norm in our experience), and who convene two or three times a year. The role played by the CAB can vary widely but generally includes discussing industry or business trends affecting the supplier or the customers' business with the supplier, current and projected uses of the supplier's products or services, market feasibility or uptake of new product ideas or innovations, emerging or changing markets, and the like.

One example of a CAB is the Lexus Owner's Advisory Forum. On a periodic basis, 15 to 20 Lexus engineers meet face to face with 15 to 20 loyal Lexus customers to discuss how the customers use their vehicles.[1] The commute to and from work, recreational uses, family considerations, vehicle performance conditions, and patterns, as well as various creature features and accessories, are all discussed openly to anticipate the next generation of vehicles and features. The Lexus Forum co-exists with a more virtual Lexus Customer

---

[1] Lucy McCauley, "How May I Help You?" *Fast Company* 32 (March 2000): 93.

Advisory Board. The Lexus CAB uses social media, online surveys, virtual and dealership-based events to stay connected to and leverage the insights of loyal Lexus owners. Customer ideas and reactions to vehicle design, customer service experiences, marketing, and customer communications are a frequent part of their customer–supplier dialogues. The Lexus CAB recently featured a "virtual lunch" with Lexus Group VP and General Manager Mark Templin, including a posting of the various Q&A from that lunch dialogue on the CAB website.

Other effective examples of deeper customer–supplier connections are joint project teams and job rotations. Joint project teams are typically teams of experts from each side of the relationship that get together, in a formal or informal fashion, to jointly work out technical or product designs, tests, problems, or ideas. Oftentimes, the teams working on these projects come together for the express purpose of the project at hand and dismantle once the project is completed. Other times, these projects, if managed appropriately, can result in ongoing joint project teams, or at least ongoing relationships between the members. As we've stated several times, any relationship between a customer and supplier representative that does not focus solely on the sales transaction can be a mutually beneficial and lasting relationship.

Job rotations are another vehicle for establishing unique and sometimes lasting relationships across the customer–supplier seam. While we don't think it happens nearly enough, we have seen examples where a member of the supplier company actually spends a period of time working with the customer company (but still on the supplier's payroll) either in an advisory capacity or shadowing their customer counterpart as he or she does their normal job. Similarly, a member of the customer company might do the same with the supplier company. Even if the exposure to the other side of the seam is only for a few weeks a year, it can be invaluable.

We've seen many supplier employees, especially technical or customer support staff, come back from such rotations with a new found appreciation for and understanding of how the supplier's products are used by or impact the customer. Conversely, we've seen many customer employees come back with a sensitivity to and appreciation for what the suppliers go through to create a good experience for the customer. Clearly, rotations can go a long way to developing valuable insights about, and stronger connections between, the various touch points of the relationship.

6

It Takes Two to Be Engaged

> - Determine who "owns" your customer focus
> - Employee engagement—vital to implementing any strategy
> - Build the capabilities needed to implement Level II

In sum, the various Level II techniques described so far are essential for converting the typical event-based, rear-view–looking, data-driven customer focus process into a more ongoing relationship-based, real-time, value-driven process. Things like touch point surveys, interviews, focus groups, on-site assessments, customer advisory boards, joint project teams, and job rotations are vital for identifying ways to make the relationship more valuable to both sides.

However, there are some drawbacks or challenges supplier companies often face as they progress to and through Level II. These include:

- The increased frequency and depth of Level II actions require more people resources than most companies have formally dedicated to their customer focus initiative.

Benefits of Touch Point Dialogues

- Goes beyond the sales transaction, metrics, and relationship managers.
- Looks at the present, not just the past.
- Multiplies and deepens the supplier's connection in the customer organization.
- Surfaces additional opportunities to differentiate the supplier company.
- Creates a more complete and informed view of what "value" means to the customer.
- Surfaces the customer's unstated needs.
- Helps identify the customer's different views of POP, POD, and UVP.
- Begins building a more pervasive sense of relationship, if not partnership.
- Can result in substantive changes (not just incremental ones) in the relationship.

- Level II touch point techniques require new skills for the suppliers' personnel and oftentimes require new skills for the customers' personnel.
- The suppliers' improved connections with their customers often reveals weak connections inside the supplier organization.
- The supplier organization is likely still defining, organizing, and managing itself around its products—not around the customer, so there's no aligned sense of customer-centric goals and urgency.
- There are still internal silos in the supplier organization that dilute or prevent an end-to-end mindset of value creation.

- Level II activities take continuous prioritizing and tenacity to develop the more complete understanding that goes beyond the sales transaction and beyond the one or two primary owners of that relationship.

The last four challenges above are all the result of a culture that hasn't yet made the adjustments it needs to really excel at its customer focus. We will be addressing these challenges in much detail later. For now, let's look more closely at the first two challenges mentioned above—insufficient resources and the lack of or need for new skills.

10-Point Customer Focus Framework

#4. Employee Engagement

Throughout the preceding discussion on touch point techniques, we stressed one important qualification that's worth repeating: Being effective at Level II requires much more than the involvement of your customer service or support staff, and it requires much more than the typical sales or account management personnel can achieve. Companies that excel in providing a consistently superior customer experience share at least one common practice: Various employees, not just those with direct customer-facing jobs, spend time interacting with customers. The more people involved in a supplier's customer focus, the more successful it can be, and the more likely it is that a genuine customer-centric culture will begin taking shape. There are two keys to enabling an effective Level II approach and eventual progress into Level III. One is to create a clear expectation for (and consistent awareness of) everyone's role in the customer focus efforts. The other is to give people the skills, tools, and support they need to successfully fulfill those expectations and roles. Let's look at each of these.

Customer Focus Cannot Be a Department or Title

Like it or not, your peoples' most common and instinctive reaction to the company's customer focus is that it's *someone else's job*. One reason for that reaction is something we discussed back in Chapter 2. The fanfare and hoopla that accompanies many customer focus efforts effectively makes it something new, something big and special . . . and unfortunately, something extra! People generally believe they already know what *their job is*, and they generally feel they already have more than enough to do. Consequently, they are quick to assume (hope) that this new initiative surely must be someone else's job.

Another reason is that one of the first things that a company wanting to kick-start or restart their customer focus does is to create a department and/or position that reinforces the notion that it's someone else's job. The minute you anoint someone as your chief customer officer, CE director, customer advocate—or any number of similar titles or roles—you've effectively shifted the responsibility from everyone to someone. One other reason for this lack of shared ownership is most companies don't take the time and care needed to help everyone understand that the customer's experience with a supplier company is influenced by all jobs—not just customer-facing jobs.

Left to their own volition, most people will move quickly to put distance between their role and any customer focus ownership and responsibility. Even people who are in customer-facing roles will instinctively try to define their responsibility and accountability for it as narrowly as possible. For example, when we are helping a company analyze and act on its customer survey results, we like to gauge the level of ownership for those results beforehand. One effective way to do this is to send a copy of your CSM survey to all (or a sampling of) your employees, and ask them to complete it in the way they believe the customer would complete it. In other words, if they were the customers, how would they rate the supplier company? Then we like to segment the results by business unit, or product line, or by region, or by functional area/department.

When we do this, we usually find similar results. One is that employees and managers (referred to collectively as "employees" from here on) often have a view of the customer's perception that is much more positive or favorable than the customer's actual view. A significant number of employees (though rarely all of them) think their company is much better at satisfying customers than it really is. The other result we consistently find is that where employees believe customer perceptions are negative, or could be improved, they typically believe the problem is due to some other department, not their department. They are quick to own responsibility for creating a favorable impression, but equally quick to disown any responsibility for negative impressions. Hard to imagine? Try it for yourself, and see what you get.

A shared sense of ownership is critical for an effective customer focus because without it, the important work to be done will fall on the shoulders of the few, instead of being shared by many. Without it, creating, deepening, maintaining, and leveraging the touch point relationships and results discussed earlier will not be possible. Without it, making the process improvements needed for a successful Level II focus, and building the cultural enablers needed at Level III, will not be possible. Key to this shared ownership is, first, ensuring clear expectations have been set; second, creating and enabling opportunities for engagement at all levels and functions; and third, ensuring there's consistent awareness of those expectations and opportunities.

Expect Everyone to Play a Role

Clear expectations begin with employees understanding the role customers play in their supplier company's world and the fact that the company exists, for no other reason, but to be a successful business by creating value for its customers. Each employee's individual job, in turn, plays a functional role in helping the company meet its customers' needs. These jobs don't exist for the sake of keeping them

Figure 6.1   Customers don't exist so employees can have jobs; Employees' jobs exist so customers can receive value.

employed, or for the sake of making them happy, or for the sake of the jobs themselves. Their jobs exist to help the company successfully deliver customer value. Figure 6.1 plainly and simply illustrates that reality. How to convey it to employees in a clear and meaningful way will be the topic for later chapters.

In this chapter, our goal is to help you understand that the customer focus will not succeed without a strong commitment to engaging employees throughout the organization around that focus.

The Customer Focus Paradox

While companies want all of their employees to own it, they tend to limit the number of employees involved in it.

As we've noted several times during our Level II discussions, enterprise value is created when customer personnel and supplier personnel engage each other at the various touch points or intersections of their respective companies. (See Figure 6.2.)

The key is to make sure all the employees and managers within the supplier circle see their roles as a critical part of enabling those who are working at the intersection. All jobs, not just the jobs in the intersection, play a role in identifying and/or delivering customer value. We get considerable pushback from naysayers who want to argue that every company has jobs that simply do not impact the customer's experience. To that we say: *Find those jobs and get rid of them!* Every job in a supplier organization either has a direct customer-facing role or, directly supports a job somewhere in the organization that is customer facing. Every job either directly or indirectly impacts the customer.

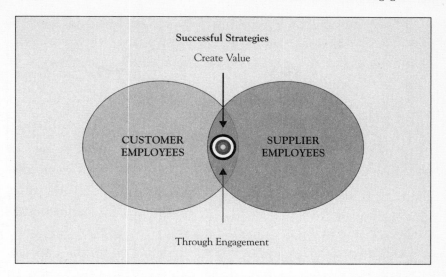

Figure 6.2   When Customer–Supplier Employees Intersect

If a job truly does neither, then we ask why it is on the payroll at all. If it's not directly or indirectly impacting the customer, the job should be eliminated, automated, or outsourced. Once we describe this to companies, it's interesting to see how eager they are to identify the customer connection to the jobs in their organizations.

Create Roles for Everyone to Play

The challenge some companies encounter is that while they want everyone to own the customer focus, they don't know how to create ways for everyone to engage in it. Our earlier touch point–teaming discussion showed a number of opportunities for supplier personnel to engage customer personnel. Below are some other examples, and in our process improvement (Step #6) and joint workout (Step #7) discussions we'll show still other opportunities companies have to get many—if not all—employees engaged in and committed to their customer focus.

Numerous examples can be found at Ritz-Carlton. The hotel chain printed its 12 "Service Values" on a laminated card carried by every employee. (See the sidebar on the Ritz-Carlton Service Values.) And while the company uses the term "service values" to

> Sears found that a 5 percent increase in its employee commitment led to a 1.8 percent increase in customer commitment and a .5 percent increase in financial results.
>
> Dave Ulrich and Norm Smallwood, *Why the Bottom Line Isn't: How to Build Value Through People and Organization* (Hoboken, NJ: John Wiley & Sons, 2003), 11.

define them, they are just as much the principles of engagement for their employees. Each day, employees of each hotel assemble for the daily "line-up." The line-up covers the key operational issues or priorities for the day and includes the "wow story" of the day, which is shared in Ritz-Carlton facilities in 21 countries. The wow story is an individual employee's example of how they wowed a customer, and how that story linked to one of the service values. As part of their customer focus, each employee is permitted to spend up to $2,000 and managers can spend up to $5,000 to avoid losing a guest.[1]

One documented example involved a family arriving at the Ritz-Carlton in Bali to discover the special milk and eggs they were transporting for their child, who had severe food allergies, had spoiled. The head chef of the hotel scoured the surrounding area for a store that carried the specialty food items, but was unsuccessful. He ultimately remembered a specialty store in Singapore, called to ensure they carried the special milk and eggs, and had his mother-in-law buy the items, jump on an airplane with them, and bring them to Bali for the family. Ritz-Carlton's "never lose a guest" principle requires setting clear expectations for their people (the 12 values), training them on how to implement those principles, and empowering them to make decisions (i.e. engage customers) within those principles.[2]

---

[1] Hal Becker, "Check into the Ritz-Carlton for Good Customer Service Tips," The Business Journals, April 22, 2008, http://www.bizjournals.com/louisville/stories/2008/04/28/smallb2.html.

[2] C. Gallo, "How Ritz-Carlton Maintains its Mystique," Businessweek.com, February 13, 2007, http://www.businessweek.com/stories/2007-02-13/how-ritz-carlton-maintains-its-mystiquebusiness week-business-news-stock-market-and-financial-advice.

Commerce Bank, headquartered in Cherry Hill, New Jersey, has a similar approach to engaging their employees around their customer focus with their Wow Team. Branches try to "out wow" each other and each year the president recognizes top performers at the company-wide Wow Awards. Their efforts include a Wow Patrol and mystery shoppers who visit each branch at least weekly to catch employees engaging the customer in ways that differentiate their bank. Branches receive ratings for the specific steps employees take to engage customers right down to the handshake and verbal greeting extended to each visitor. Without their customer-focused culture and employees who are hired, trained, and rewarded to engage and wow customers, Commerce believes it would quickly become just another bank. They actually have something called a "Kill a Stupid Rule" program. If an employee identifies a rule that prevents them from wowing customers, the bank pays them $50. Imagine that . . . encouraging—even rewarding—employees for finding rules that need abolished. Wow![3]

Training is one area that surprises us as to how underutilized it is as an employee–customer engagement vehicle. At Motorola University, for example, 45 percent of the training participants are not Motorola personnel, but are customers and suppliers who are invited to attend as a way to build their skills and knowledge and to further reinforce a mutually loyal relationship. Similarly, General Electric's (GE) Crotonville, New York, training and development center provides as much training to customers and key suppliers as it does to GE personnel.[4] Whirlpool offers customers, among other participants, management and technical training. A division of Greyhound that serves the airlines industry provides customers with safety and flight service training. And Marriott Corporation provides specialized training to selected customers.[5]

---

[3] Chuck Salter, "Customer Service: Commerce Bank," *Fast Company* 58 (May 2002): 80.

[4] Ron Ashkenas et al., *The Boundaryless Organization: Breaking the Chains of Organizational Structure*, rev ed. (San Francisco: Jossey-Bass, 2002), 84.

[5] Ron Ashkenas et al., *The Boundaryless Organization: Breaking the Chains of Organizational Structure*, (San Francisco: Jossey-Bass, 1995), 204.

The value and impact of these training approaches cannot be overstated. They can present unique and powerful supplier opportunities for your organization in several ways:

- You have direct dialogues with and gain unique insights from your customers.
- You further raise their comfort with, and trust and confidence in, your personnel.
- You engage them in forward-looking conversations about industry trends.
- You reinforce the sense of how important they are to you.
- You indirectly showcase your own expertise or offerings.
- You develop new personal connections that can be further leveraged over time.

One other area that is not exploited nearly enough is taking plant tours or site visits of your customers' facilities or operations. Usually, when a supplier does this, it's done at the management level, or involves a narrow slice of supplier personnel such as those involved in sales, quality assurance, or product development. These kinds of visits, however, are invaluable opportunities to expose *all* of your company's personnel—customer facing or not—to your customer's business. I have yet to see a customer balk at the idea of having an administrative, front-line, or back office employee join a tour of their facility. It's always the supplier that either doesn't consider the possibilities, or doesn't want to "impose" on the customer. That's a weak answer in our view. For every reason you think you can't or shouldn't do this, there are probably three reasons why you should. This isn't something you do all at once or make a big deal of. You work at it steadily, and quietly, over time. For every customer tour or site visit you make, ensure just one (at a minimum) non–customer-facing employee is part of the touring group. How hard can that be? Over time, you'll be able to expose a significant number of your employees to the customer who wouldn't have otherwise ever seen or had a chance to appreciate the reason for your company existing. If you have any doubt about the impact this can have on your employees—try it . . . just once . . . and see for yourself.

One final engagement example we want to mention and have successfully introduced to many companies is to designate someone in each department, functional area, business unit, or other appropriate entity as the customer focus point person. Organizations call them by various names: customer focus liaisons, customer focus coordinators, customer experience advocates, customer experience champions, or something similar. Their specific customer focus responsibilities will vary from one company to another, but generally consist of the following more common ones:

- Serve as an advocate and source of the most up-to-date information about the customer focus in general.

- Act as a conduit that ensures two-way communications between the colleagues in their respective department or work area and the customer focus leaders, steering team, or senior leadership.

- Test ideas and act as a sounding board for the customer focus team that considers and plans the implementation steps of the journey.

- Coordinate or spearhead the implementation of any specific steps or projects that involve or impact their respective department or work area.

- Serve as the touch point owner who coordinates any customer focus activity, including the joint projects we'll discuss later, for a given touch point, process, or function.

These assignments are not full-time responsibilities but are performed as part of the individual's normal job responsibilities. The more people involved, the smaller the demand on their time. There is, however, an extra level of work for these people to do—even if only minor effort is involved. Given that added effort, one particularly effective approach is to assign these liaison roles to high-potential (Hi-Po) performers or to individuals who are being groomed for future management roles or are participating in what some companies refer to as their leadership development program (LDP). People in Hi-Po or LDP programs are typically willing to stretch their responsibilities, tend to enjoy high-visibility assignments, are generally interested in progressive leadership and best practices, and are usually looking for ways to raise their level of contribution to the organization. They are oftentimes a natural fit for customer focus special assignments or informal leadership roles.

Ritz-Carlton's 12 Service Values

1. I build strong relationships and create Ritz-Carlton guests for life.
2. I am always responsive to the expressed and unexpressed wishes and needs of our guests.
3. I am empowered to create unique, memorable, and personal experiences for our guests.
4. I understand my role in achieving the Key Success Factors, embracing Community Footprints, and creating The Ritz-Carlton Mystique.
5. I continuously seek opportunities to innovate and improve the Ritz-Carlton experience.
6. I own and immediately resolve guest problems.
7. I create a work environment of teamwork and lateral service so that the needs of our guests and each other are met.
8. I have the opportunity to continuously learn and grow.
9. I am involved in the planning of the work that affects me.

10. I am proud of my professional appearance, language, and behavior.

11. I protect the privacy and security of our guests, my fellow employees, and the company's confidential information and assets.

12. I am responsible for uncompromising levels of cleanliness and creating a safe and accident-free environment.

In reviewing the above 12 service values, you'll note some clear parallels with parts of our discussion thus far.

- Value #1—guests for life—speaks to the quest for loyalty and lifetime value (LTV).

- Value #2—expressed and unexpressed wishes and needs get to the unstated needs of Level II.

- Value #3—creating unique, personal experiences is consistent with finding those touch point unique value propositions (UVP) we seek at Level II.

- Value #6—I own guest problems. (In other words, all employees own customer satisfaction.)

While it is vital to set clear expectations about who owns the customer focus and who is expected to engage around that focus (i.e., everyone!), equally important is ensuring everyone is consistently and continually kept aware of those expectations.

Maintaining Awareness of Expectations and Opportunities

A critical misstep by many companies is underestimating what it takes for employees to really embrace and execute on initiatives that come down from above. Just because the company's senior leaders issue a charge or declare their commitment to something, that doesn't mean the rest of the organization will rally around, embrace, and implement it. Nothing could be further from reality. If anything, the opposite is just as likely to happen—anything ranging from giving the project lip service support, to benign neglect, to outright resistance. Over the years we have seen literally hundreds of initiatives, campaigns, and programs that are born at the executive level but die at the entry level. One of the key reasons is the grassroots implementers—the managers and employees who must operationalize the executive edict—have not been engaged at the outset and throughout the implementation.

Let's look at a recent example of a company that was in year five of its customer focus initiative, but was puzzled by the mixed results. First, this company had been conducting customer satisfaction surveys and employee satisfaction surveys for five years. To its credit, the company knew there was a linkage between satisfied employees and satisfied customers and wanted to track, evaluate, and improve its internal and external activities accordingly. For the five-year period, the company's employee satisfaction ratings continually improved to a five-year peak of 89 percent satisfaction—an enviable score by any standard. However, during that same five-year period, their customer satisfaction scores were relatively flat. Any gains in certain satisfaction factors, customer segments, or parts of the business were offset by lower ratings in a different set of satisfaction factors, segments, or other parts of the business. To further aggravate its senior leaders, the company's economic growth indicators during the five-year period were clearly trending down. Not a financial disaster by any means, but very much an unexpected downward trend that raised questions, if not concerns.

We were asked to help the company evaluate and improve its situation. Among the first things we did was shift its focus from employee satisfaction to employee engagement. We have rarely seen a company in which the employees—in general—don't feel they are overworked or underpaid. There is always going to be some segment of employees, in some segment of the company, who are unhappy about some aspect of their employment. We're not suggesting that employee happiness isn't important, but we are saying it's not sufficient. If you strive for satisfied or happy employees, that may or may not improve your performance in the customer marketplace. But if you strive for employees who are engaged—specifically around the customer's experience—that will most likely impact your marketplace performance.

We replaced the company's 40-question employee satisfaction survey with a 15-question employee–customer experience engagement survey. Those 15 questions were rolled up to form a three-factor engagement composite score in each of the following three factors:

Q1–5. I know how the company's customer experience (CE) strategy can benefit the company's business performance and earnings, and my personal performance and earnings.

Q6–10. I understand the way(s) my individual job, role, or position supports that CE strategy.

Q11–15. I have the tools, training, and/or support I need to perform effectively in the CE elements of my role.

The resulting composite engagement score was as instructive as it was irritating. (See Figure 6.3.)

Simply put, more than three-fourths (36 percent + 41 percent = 77 percent) of this company's employees didn't understand, know their role in, or feel equipped to support the company's CE strategy. They weren't engaged. When an organization's people are engaged

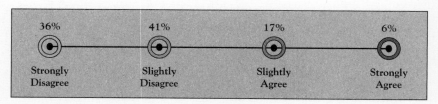

| 36% | 41% | 17% | 6% |
| Strongly Disagree | Slightly Disagree | Slightly Agree | Strongly Agree |

Figure 6.3 Composite Score for Employee–Customer Experience Engagement

with a particular effort, it means they are enlightened about, embrace, and are willing to execute it.

Enlightened—I get it; I intellectually understand it.

Embracing—I support it; I am motivated by it.

Executing—I do it; I am physically engaged in it.

That kind of engagement is vital and is not going to happen without each manager and employee (1) understanding what type and level of engagement is expected of them; (2) being provided and shown how to take advantage of the various opportunities to be engaged; and (3) being continually reminded of those expectations and opportunities, as well as being reinforced for doing their part. More about reinforcing and reminding will be discussed in the "consequences" and "change" sections of the 10-Point Customer Focus Framework.

Before leaving this discussion of employee engagement, let's look at a tool that can be quite effective at the early stages of a customer focus journey. It's sometimes called a Customer Experience Readiness Survey, an Awareness Survey, or a Cultural Baseline Survey and is intended to accomplish the following objectives, among others:

- Assess how effectively communications are reaching or taking root in various levels and parts of the organization.

- Determine the organization's current view of customer satisfaction.

- Gauge the level of importance or necessity people attribute to the customer focus.

- Assess whether people grasp how the customer focus benefits the business and/or them personally.

- Generally gauge the level of acceptance or resistance the company might expect or be experiencing.

- Establish a baseline measure that can be used to track, evaluate, and correct progress.

Sample Customer Experience Readiness Survey

Based on your personal familiarity with our Customer Focus initiative, please check the number at the right that best describes your view in each of the areas below. Please read the rating scale for each question as some may differ, and note that a rating of "0" denotes Uncertain or Not Applicable.		Check One				
		1	2	3	4	0
1	I believe the quality of service my department currently provides to <u>external</u> customers is: 1 = Marginal; 2 = Adequate; 3 = Good; 4 = Excellent; 0 = Uncertain/not applicable					
2	I believe the quality of service the Company currently provides to <u>external</u> customers is: 1 = Marginal; 2 = Adequate; 3 = Good; 4 = Excellent; 0 = Uncertain/not applicable					
3	I can explain the difference between a satisfied customer and a loyal customer. 1 = Strongly Disagree; 2 = Disagree; 3 = Agree; 4 = Strongly Agree; 0 = Uncertain					
4	I understand the key aspects of the Company's Customer Focus initiative—that is, I can describe the key aspects of the initiative to others. 1 = Strongly Disagree; 2 = Disagree; 3 = Agree; 4 = Strongly Agree; 0 = Uncertain					
5	I know how the Customer Focus initiative connects to the Company's business plan and its other business priorities. 1 = Strongly Disagree; 2 = Disagree; 3 = Agree; 4 = Strongly Agree; 0 = Uncertain					
6	The Company clearly needs the Customer Focus initiative. 1 = Strongly Disagree; 2 = Disagree; 3 = Agree; 4 = Strongly Agree; 0 = Uncertain					
7	I understand my department's role in implementing the Customer Focus initiative. 1 = Strongly Disagree; 2 = Disagree; 3 = Agree; 4 = Strongly Agree; 0 = Uncertain					
8	I know what I must personally do in my role to help implement the Customer Focus initiative. 1 = Strongly Disagree; 2 = Disagree; 3 = Agree; 4 = Strongly Agree; 0 = Uncertain					
9	I understand how I will personally benefit if the Company meets its Customer Focus objectives. 1 = Strongly Disagree; 2 = Disagree; 3 = Agree; 4 = Strongly Agree; 0 = Uncertain					
10	COMMENTS: Please let us know of any other viewpoints, ideas, or reactions you have that might help us more effectively meet our Customer Focus objectives.					

Figure 6.4   Sample Customer Experience Readiness Survey

Sample Customer Experience Readiness Survey

Figure 6.4 is a very basic version of a customer experience readiness survey that is generic enough to apply to a broad range of industries and cultures. In practice, we would use a survey that is highly tailored to the particular organization's unique culture, challenges, and objectives.

As mentioned in our strategy discussion, a company's customer focus should raise the bar on what the supplier wants and tries to achieve. It will

Scan for printable copy

most likely raise the customers' expectations of what more might be possible, and given the types of engagement we've been discussing, it will certainly raise the bar on the types of skills and capabilities the supplier needs to progress.

That's why training and tools are considered a key element for a successful customer focus. You'll have people engaging the customer who might not have done so historically. You'll have customer-facing people getting involved in ways they haven't yet been involved. And you'll have everyone focused on understanding, embracing, and implementing a more customer-centric culture or mindset. This will require new skills for any number of people.

10-Point Customer Focus Framework

#5. Training and Tools

So here are some questions you'll need to work through to ensure you are "tooled up" to execute your plan. Given your company's customer focus:

- What are the top priorities or initiatives the company plans to pursue?
- What capabilities does the company need (broadly) to achieve those priorities?
- What training and tools do those who must implement these priorities need?

Over the years, we have come to see a recurring theme in the capabilities and skills companies need to implement their customer focus priorities. Listed in Figure 6.5 are six of the more common customer focus capabilities on which many companies concentrate. Also listed in Figure 6.5 are some representative, individual competencies or skills that often align with or enable those broader

Company-wide Capabilities	Individual Competencies (Skills)		
Product or Service Innovation	Creative Thinking	Pattern Recognition	Problem Solving
Speed to Market	Decision Quality	Priority Setting	Rapid Learning
Shifting Brand Preference	Influencing Others	Understanding Others	Customer Orientation
Continuous Improvement	Dealing with Ambiguity	Personal Development	Process Orientation
Consultative Selling	Active Listening	Command Skills	Collaborative Negotiation
Optimizing Performance	Action Orientation	Managing & Measuring Work	Drive for Results

Figure 6.5   Company Capabilities and Employee Skills

capabilities. The competencies or skills listed are not in any way meant to be exhaustive or absolute—they are offered as typical examples. There are many other individual competencies or skills that could apply to any given organization.

Some of those individual skills are best learned on the job, where others can be taught in formal training settings. Figure 6.6 shows some of the specific training courses typically needed and used by supplier companies—many of which are provided both internally to managers and employees, and externally to selected customer personnel.

MOST COMMON TRAINING COURSES	
Creative Thinking & Innovation Techniques	Group Problem Solving
Process Improvement Methods and Tools	Solutions Selling or Consultative Selling
Facilitation Skills	Customer Service & Recovery Techniques
Conflict Resolution	Collaborative Negotiations
Building & Deploying High-Performing Teams	Project Management Methods and Tools
Change Management	Business Acumen/Business Fundamentals

Figure 6.6   Training Courses Typically Needed and Used

The value of some of the courses shown in Figure 6.6 will become clearer when we talk about Process Orientation Step #7 of the framework. While all of these courses can play and have played an important role in equipping a company's employees to execute their customer focus responsibilities, the Business Acumen or Fundamentals of Business course is of particular importance. It's not so much a specific skill that employees use in their daily jobs, as much as it is an effective foundational course that helps them better appreciate the customer focus and put it in the proper context.

In essence, this foundation course is designed to provide employees, in fairly basic terms and examples, with four core teachings:

How the company makes money—turning income into profits.

How the customer impacts the company's profits—including customer revenue and customer-related expenses.

How employees impact the customer's spending—including quality, service, brand, and price variables.

How that spending impacts employees' earnings and opportunities—such as base pay, incentives, benefits, job stability, career growth, and so on.

These basic business courses can also reinforce the fact that many different functions or departments impact the customer, and the customer, in turn, impacts employee earnings and opportunities. Such courses often include a nontechnical picture or diagram, along with explanations, depicting the company's basic business model, which further helps employees visualize how they fit into the business. (See Figure 6.7 for a very basic business model example.)

Obviously, training in and of itself doesn't automatically translate directly into new or changed skills, performance, or behavior. It's the practical application of that training to real work situations that we seek. And that's where tools can play an important role. They can serve as practice aids or reference guides that help personnel remember or resort to what they learned in the training.

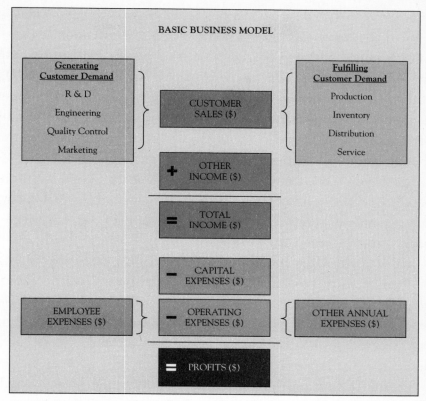

Note: The above business model was used purely as a demonstration for an employee training program. It was not intended to be a technically complete or precise model.

Figure 6.7   The Basic Business Model

Questionnaires for the on-site assessments or touch point interviews described earlier, dialogue and recovery scripts, sales playbooks, retention risk review guides, and other field guides and tools have been developed and used by many companies to support their people as they apply newly learned customer focus techniques to their jobs.

Another important category includes the more technology-based tools that support people in the execution of their customer focus responsibilities. Tech-tools such as customer relationship management (CRM) systems, customer analytics applications, price modeling tools, customer service web portals, customer service representative (CSR) agent stations, and the like can all play critical roles in your customer focus. The types and sophistication of these tools, technology-based or otherwise, vary widely and are beyond the scope of this book. But as one example (not technology-based), we have frequently used what we call the Customer Focus Compass as an effective field practice aid for customer-focused employees. It provides a model they can use to think through and follow-up on the implications of various customer focus problems or situations.

See Figure 6.8 for one version of the compass. When we train people how to use it, we typically provide them with several different customer experience scenarios and have them dissect the scenario using the compass.

For example, when confronted with a situation, customer insight, or observation, first look north or think about how the situation links upward to the broader customer focus or business strategy. Is it consistent with or conflicting with the company's customer focus strategy or key principles? Will resolution of the issue advance the strategy, dilute it, or not impact it either way?

Then look west (or think backward) to what might have caused or created the situation or question. Is there an underlying policy, process, or practice—or the interpretation or implementation

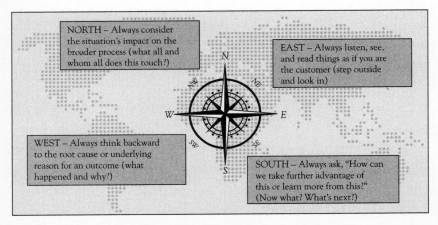

Figure 6.8　Customer Focus Compass

thereof—that might need to be evaluated, reaffirmed, or revised to ensure it's still relevant, current, or effective?

Look east (or think ahead) about if or how other customers might be experiencing this particular situation. Is it isolated to this one customer, to a particular type of customers, or many types of customers? Does it concern one product or service, an entire product line, or all products? If a change were made to address the situation at hand, how might it impact others? What—if any—of those others should be conferred with before or while making the change?

Finally, look south (or below the surface) to see how we can extend the benefit of this learning or fix. How can we replicate it or further leverage it into other products, customer segments, divisions, or regions? How can we multiply or maximize the benefit or gain we get from it?

CHAPTER

7

Customer Focus Is a Process—Not an Event

- Ten common derailers of the customer focus journey
- The role, mindset, and discipline of process improvement
- Customer–Supplier Workouts—Value Chain Labs®

We've mentioned before that launching and sustaining the customer focus journey is not for the faint of heart. Just like any business strategy, staying the course requires a company to anticipate and be ready to decisively address the obstacles that will arise over time. One thing we too frequently see companies do at the outset, which creates a self-inflicted obstacle, is to call their customer focus a program, initiative, project, campaign, or some other seemingly *temporary* endeavor. These terms or labels paint the entirely wrong picture and create the wrong expectations. Moreover, these labels are often associated with the same derailers or pitfalls that cause such events, or initiatives du jour, to end up on the program scrap pile. As mentioned earlier, a number of people will instinctively look for ways to distance themselves from anything they view as a flash-in-the-pan event. They feel that, like so many other prior initiatives, this one too shall pass. *I outlasted this company's last "brilliant idea," and I'll outlast this one.* That's one reason why we very purposefully refer to customer focus as a journey or a process.

> Customer focus is a process . . . not an event. When companies treat it like an event, the results are going to be . . . uneventful!

Regardless of what you call it and how enduring your resolve is to see it through, moving from Level I to Level II will require you to anticipate and manage some key derailers or momentum killers. Over the years, we've come to realize there are a number of recurring actions—no matter the label you choose to describe them—that typically cause a company's customer focus to stall, particularly at Level II (if not Level I). The 10 derailers we most frequently see are:

---

10 Common Customer Focus Derailers

1. Not tying customer focus to the business strategy (seeing it instead as an isolated or extra layer of work)
2. Picking the wrong customers to focus on (limited or no return on your effort)
3. Not prioritizing segments, channels, customers, or issues (trying to do it all at once)
4. Assuming you know how to satisfy customers without asking them

5. Asking for customer input but not acting on it—whether it's positive or negative input

6. Not investing in building or acquiring vital skills or tools

7. Not measuring and showcasing progress—including economic results

8. Focusing on blame instead of continuous learning and improvement

9. Senior leaders abdicating responsibility and ownership

10. Senior leaders tolerating interference or resistance

We've already discussed the first six derailers, and hope you are now better positioned to address them—if not anticipate and avoid them in the first place. We will address the last four derailers as we proceed through the Level III steps and techniques.

One other critically important obstacle is the failure to understand and treat customer focus as a process. While process is inferred in several of the above derailers, we want to discuss it separately and more fully because of the role it plays. Specifically, there are two factors that underscore its significance. One is the fact that customer focus is a process and, as such, does not have a completion date. The customer's definition of and need for value is not a finite or stationary target. There are aspects of it that won't change very much or very often, but other aspects of it will continually morph and evolve. Like you, your customers have their own markets and customers that they serve. As their customers grow, shrink, and change, so too will the resultant needs of your customers as they respond to those changes.

In addition, your competition is not going to idly sit by and watch you tighten your grip on your customers without putting up a fight. Whatever unique value you provide your customers will eventually become the target others are aiming at. And they're not aiming to just hit it, but to shoot through and surpass it.

> *As soon as you build a bigger and better mousetrap to sell,*
> *some competitor will develop a bigger and stronger mouse.*
> —*Unknown*

Competitive advantage has a shelf life, and it's only a matter of time until today's point of differentiation becomes tomorrow's point of parity. You can't sit still. You must continue finding ways to be unique. In sum, the steps of understanding and providing customer value form a continuous process that can never be considered "finished."

The other important reason for viewing customer focus as a process is because it is actually a series of processes and subprocesses. Whether we're talking about the sales process, production and quality assurance processes, order entry and fulfillment, installation and service, credit, claims, or warranties—they are *all* processes. The purpose of Level I is to find out (detect) what aspects of those processes are stopping you from meeting the customers' expectations and needs as desired. Level I almost always results in a supplier discovering a process that's broken, not working optimally, doesn't yet exist, or is not integrated as well as it could be with other internal processes. It's vital that a supplier company understands, and knows how to evaluate and improve its processes.

Level II is geared to learning more about the customer's internal processes that touch your processes so you can discover ways to deliver value that's greater, faster, or better than what you currently deliver or what the competition can deliver. Level II is less about fixing processes, and more about aligning and integrating them with the customer's processes—thus optimizing them. The need to understand and optimize processes is even more critical at this level than it is at Level I.

In short, no customer focus journey is going to go very far or be very successful without the supplier company, and possibly certain customers, closely examining their related processes and making fundamental changes or improvements to the way they function and support one another. Step #6 of our 10-point framework addresses this process orientation and deals with several different aspects or dimensions of it.

10-Point Customer Focus Framework

#6. Process Orientation

Value Chain and Business Modeling

One aspect of process orientation we urge organizations to focus on is in helping your employees understand the company's position in the broader value chain or value creation process. It's surprising how many employees, even sales personnel, don't know how their company's products or services are used in their customers' businesses. And it's also helpful for employees to have a general sense of how the company's supply chain affects its ability to meet customer needs. Generally describing or illustrating the broader value chain to them also reinforces the fact that your company doesn't exist in a vacuum or for its own sake. It exists only insofar as there are customers to buy your products or services. And you can provide those products or services only insofar as you have the right supply chain supporting you. Figure 7.1 illustrates a basic and generic value chain that we've had companies build out and tailor to their respective customer and supplier segments.

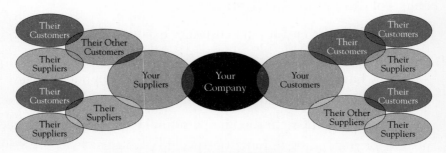

Figure 7.1   A Basic Value Chain

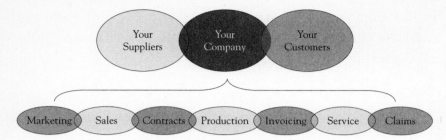

Figure 7.2   An End-to-End Process for Creating Customer Value

We're not talking about trying to make your employees experts in this area, but just generating their broad appreciation for it can be helpful. We'll talk more about the value chain perspective and implications at Level III.

Many companies go further than this and actually map out their key business processes or functional areas to show how they connect to each end of the value chain. (See Figure 7.2.) Again, this is a very basic illustration of what we mean. It is not intended to be a technical mapping and explanation of a formal business model.

Mapping Customer Focus Pivot Points

Another aspect of process we view as important is to identify and portray how the various supplier functions, processes, or people actually touch the customer's functions, processes, or people. The benefits of these process maps are to:

- Document the end-to-end customer experience with the supplier company.

- Show how specific functions or roles in the supplier company affect the customer experience.

- Identify who the right supplier personnel (touch point owners) are for responding to function-specific problems or opportunities revealed through the supplier's VOC efforts.

CE PIVOT POINTS – Version A

**Figure 7.3   Customer Experience Pivots from
Point to Point, Version A**

The level of detail we've seen used in these customer experience or focus maps can vary widely from company to company. Some companies document their map only at a very high level—portraying only the macro processes or steps in the customer's experience. We often refer to these macro steps as *pivot points* because they represent points where the customer's experience or the supplier's focus significantly shifts, or pivots, between key processes, functions, or steps. (See Figure 7.3.)

In Figure 7.3, the arrow labeled *First Impressions* represents any steps or activities designed to promote the brand or generate customer demand, such as market research, marketing, advertising, and other indirect selling activities. The arrow labeled *Pre-Sale Activities* refers to all direct selling activities or steps up to and resulting in a closed sale. The term *Manage/Meet Expectations* includes everything from formally closing the sale to delivering, servicing, and supporting the resulting customer order or account. And the final arrow in this example, labeled *Leverage Loyalty*, refers to repeat sales efforts, cross-selling or up-selling efforts, generating customer referrals, and securing customer testimonials. That last pivot point is one that most companies don't consciously, proactively, or sufficiently address. We'll talk about that more in Level III.

Version B (see Figure 7.4) of our pivot point diagram shows another example of macro level touch (pivot) points labeled with more self-explanatory terms across the spectrum of the customer experience: *sales visit, purchase, financing,* and *service.*

This last example, Version C (see Figure 7.5), is a more granular and comprehensive view that looks at the customer's experience but

**Figure 7.4   Customer Experience Pivots from
Point to Point, Version B**

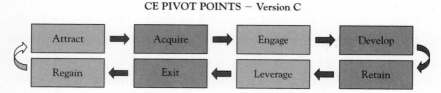

**Figure 7.5   Customer Experience Pivots from
Point to Point, Version C**

more from the supplier's perspective or focus. *Attract*, *Acquire*, and *Retain* are straightforward terms. *Engage* refers to what this company would be doing to create the deeper relationships and barriers to entry we've already discussed. *Develop* refers to the supplier's efforts to further penetrate the customer's share of wallet (SOW) (i.e., develop or grow the account). *Leverage* in this example is very similar to the *Leverage Loyalty* step described in Version A. *Exit* includes customers who left on their own as well as customers whom the supplier wanted to leave and may have forced, helped, or "allowed" to leave. And the *regain* step reflects any efforts to win back a customer who has defected.

Mapping Customer Experience Touch Points

Touch point maps are typically more detailed than the pivot point maps discussed earlier, and as such include significantly more process and subprocess steps. Each touch point usually represents discrete, readily discernible tasks and activities that take place at various points of the customer's experience. Some companies map every single touch point that exists, while others map only the more critical touch points or *anticipate moments*. These are the touch points where customer value can be either created or destroyed, or be either improved or diluted. In short, anticipate moments are the touch points that make a real difference in the customer's experience and view of the supplier, and as such significantly differentiate the supplier (negatively or positively) from the customer's other suppliers.

The customer experience touch point map shown in Figure 7.6 is for a software development company. Across the top horizontal axis, you'll see four pivot points: *Pre-Sale, Sale, Install,* and *Support*. Under each pivot point you'll see the touch points making up each pivot point, with each touch point representing a specific process, task, or activity that involves or impacts the customer. The vertical axis on the left represents the company's various departments or functional areas. The cells formed by the resulting matrix are then used to reflect each department's role (D = direct impact; I = indirect impact; blank cell = no impact) in engaging the customer at each respective touch point.

Process orientation isn't as much about mapping processes as it is a mindset and discipline of identifying, evaluating, informing, and improving them. We have taken time to delve into value chain and touch point mapping a bit because it is often the starting point for any process evaluation and improvement effort, and it can play a significant role in helping everyone see the customer's role in the company's business, and the employee's role in the customer's experience. The maps, as tools in and'of themselves, are quite informative and instructive. The real gains in effectiveness and efficiency, however, come from improving your processes.

Below are just two of the myriad documented examples of customer-driven process improvements.

GE Appliances (GEA) and Sears (who sold certain General Electric brands and had become GEA's largest customer) joined together to examine their mutual processes and relationships in five key areas: appliance delivery, billing procedures, inventory management, in-store merchandising, and customer and market information. Together they questioned procedures that had outlived

CUSTOMER TOUCH POINT MAP	Pre-Sale				Sale		Install							Support								
	Gather Requirements	Cold Call	Concept Presentation	Technical Demo	Terms & Conditions	Software Invoicing	Kick-off Call	Customer Orientation	Build Database	Maintenance	Installation	Support Invoicing	User Training	Support Calls	Software Issues	Added SWD; Testing	Additional Training	Contract Negotiation	IT Consulting	Customer Care Cases	Special Conversions	Support System I/O
Sales	I	D	D	D	D	I		I			I							I	I	D		
Finance	D				D	D						D						D				I
S/W Development	D		D	I			D	D			I				D	D	D		I	I	D	
Quality Assurance	I		I	I				I			I			I	D	D			I	I	D	I
Training	I		I	I			D						D				D				D	I
Tech Support	I	I	D	I			I	D	I	D	D	D		D	D	I	D	D	D	D	D	D
Human Resources				I						I	I		D				I		D			
MIS	I			D	I	D			D	I		D		I			I				I	D
Product Management	D	I	D	D			I	D		I	D			I	I	D		D	I	I	I	

Figure 7.6 Customer Experience Touch Point Map

their usefulness, looked for ways to remove the redundancy in their mutual processes, and tried to reduce the relationship to its most essential factors or drivers. The results of this early effort between the two companies set the stage for a broader, longer-term joint focus on production, sales, and inventory.[1]

Another example came from the fiberglass products group of PPG Industries. The fiberglass group was working with an automotive parts manufacturer who was developing a fiberglass-reinforced plastic suspension spring for a major automobile manufacturer. But PPG encountered problems when no matter how they formulated the fiberglass, the customer was not able to create a strong enough bond between PPG's fiberglass component and the parts manufacturer's plastic materials. After a series of product failures, the two sides (PPG and their parts manufacturer customer) reached an unusual agreement. The customer would help PPG re-create their proprietary bonding process within PPG, and they would work together to test different fiberglass components using the customer's bonding process under varying conditions. The effort resulted in a successful new application for fiberglass that would later expand beyond the automobile model it was initially planned for.[2]

And one final example that we were recently personally involved with pertained to a global supplier (let's call them ABC Inc.) who was servicing a global energy company, but was only serving a small percentage of the energy company's total operations (i.e., the energy company only used ABC Inc. in 20 percent of the countries where they both conducted business). The supplier wanted to identify and improve the processes that the energy company felt were key to expanding ABC's business with more of the energy company's locations. Working together, they identified two specific processes one

---

[1] Dave Ulrich, Steve Kerr, and Ron Ashkenas, *The GE Work-Out: How to Implement GE's Revolutionary Method for Busting Bureaucracy & Attacking Organizational Problems* (New York: McGraw-Hill, 2002), 206.

[2] Ron Ashkenas et al., *The Boundaryless Organization: Breaking the Chains of Organizational Structure,* (San Francisco: Jossey-Bass, 1995), 238.

or both sides could improve to increase the suppliers' business in other countries. One process was the customer's demand forecasting system. It was very inconsistent from country to country, causing dramatic and quick (unexpected) changes in inventory levels for ABC. This often caused missed delivery dates for the customer, and significant costs to ABC as the company was forced to quickly switch the destinations of major deliveries.

The other issue they jointly identified as a problem was ABC's process of informing their own facilities in different countries about the availability of new services or products, and how existing customers in that country could leverage the new services and products. For example, ABC had a new technology that allowed customers to use a cheaper and safer product in conjunction with one of ABC's services. The new technology had been launched in the United States, was in the process of launching in Western Europe, but had not been launched or even communicated yet to ABC's facilities in the Middle East. When the customer's plant manager in the Middle East heard about the technology, but didn't know it was from ABC Inc., the plant manager unknowingly started calling around to various suppliers to see if he could get access to the new offering. Unfortunately, a competitor of ABC was able to convince the plant manager that they could match the lower price of ABC's improved offering, and the plant manager agreed to a six-month contract with the competitor. Had ABC's Middle East team members known about the new technology launch, they would have been able to keep the competitor out of the picture. Now, both sides have agreed to look at ways to be more transparent in their evolving needs and solutions, but still protect their respective needs for confidentiality and intellectual property protection.

These are just a few examples of the process improvements that can be discovered and implemented to improve a supplier's business outcomes.

Before we leave this discussion of process orientation, we'll offer one other tool that has helped a number of companies. When a supplier company is in Level II and has a voice of the customer (VOC) process comprised of multiple listening posts, and is making progress at deepening the insights and foothold gained at various touch points in the customer organization, they'll not lack for things to address. To the contrary, there will be more ideas, opportunities, and challenges than the supplier company will be able to feasibly tackle at any given time. Prioritizing is very important. There are many ways companies can prioritize the order in which they'll pursue various process improvement challenges and opportunities, and all of them serve a purpose.

We like to use a model that identifies the challenges and opportunities that are most important in two respects. One is the degree to which they represent a problem, weakness, or risk to your *customer* portfolio. The other is the degree to which they link directly to your existing business *strategy*. The Value Driver Priority Matrix (see Figure 7.7) can be used to plot your long "to-do" list and prioritize it based on their customer–strategy connection.

The intent of the Value Driver Priority Matrix is to help a company prioritize those actions that build the most value for the most stakeholders. In this tool, we assume the key stakeholder groups are the company's customers (horizontal axis at the bottom) and the other stakeholders served by the company's strategy (vertical axis at the left). The supplier's long list of actions, gleaned from their VOC efforts or extended Level II touch point efforts, are plotted on the matrix based on whether they represent something customers are very satisfied with (high) or very unsatisfied with (low); and whether the action has a low or high degree of linkage to or alignment with the company's business strategy (or operating plan in some cases).

The quadrants in this particular version are explained as follows:

A. Actions with high strategic alignment and low customer satisfaction should be top priority actions as they stand to deliver the most gains—or minimize the greatest risks—if they are corrected, improved, or implemented, whatever the case may be.

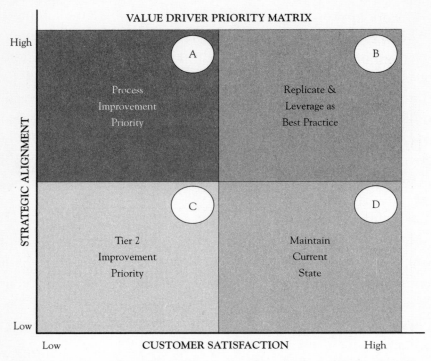

**Figure 7.7   The Value Driver Priority Matrix Helps Rank
Your Priorities**

They also typically require substantial effort, time, or money
to address. This is what we call the High Effort–High Gain
quadrant.

B. Actions with high strategic alignment and high customer satisfaction should be the next area of focus because the company
is already doing them well in certain areas. Reaping the added
gains of doing them well across the entire enterprise or customer base is more a matter of replicating and further leveraging that which you already know how to do well. This is the
Low Effort–High Gain quadrant.

C. Actions with low strategic alignment and low customer satisfaction are the next level priority. The reason they are lower
priority than quadrant B actions is that they may make it
harder to create buy-in throughout the company given their
lower strategic linkage. They're more apt to be viewed as extra

work or non-strategic. Therefore, the work involved to gain traction internally while raising efficacy externally can be significant. You normally wouldn't want these actions competing for the attention of quadrant A and B actions, which usually yield proportionately more gain for the effort expended. This is the High Effort–Low Gain quadrant.

D. These are your lowest level of priority actions to focus on because the customer is already happy with you in these areas, and there is nothing strategically driving attention to these actions. As a result, you would be hard-pressed to convince anyone internally to invest any urgency or resources to these actions. That is not to suggest you can afford to let these areas slip in efficacy. They must, at a minimum, be maintained. This is called the Low Effort–Low Gain quadrant.

The process orientation we just discussed clearly creates work for any supplier company committed to reaching the increasing profitability the customer focus journey can bring. We have rarely heard a company (supplier or customer) tell us that the process improvement efforts they undertook weren't worthwhile.

That's not to say some don't come away disappointed. Most often, those who are disappointed by these efforts come up short for one of two reasons. One is that they approached process improvement as a quick fix exercise and didn't commit to doing it well the first time. This includes failing to flush out and fix root causes, not engaging customers at appropriate stages or decision points, or underestimating the amount of cultural change or resistance certain process improvements might require.

The other typical reason some are disappointed by process improvement initiatives is their reluctance or inability to make tough decisions along the way. For example, you can't build or improve a process and not have people who are willing and able to support it. Companies too often try to "bend" a process around their problem performers rather than move these performers out of the way. Another example is not being willing to deal with sacred cows such as a process that was put in place by a legacy member of the company. If it is no longer relevant or effective it needs to be shut down or improved—regardless of whose brainchild or pet project it was. Another sacred cow we often encounter is a process that was created or changed to satisfy a large customer but requires more work than that customer's business with you would justify. That process either needs to be changed or the customer beneficiary needs to absorb the cost of continuing it.

For the most part, however, companies come away from most process improvement efforts admitting that they are better off after than they were before they undertook the effort. Even though it does create work, that work can often be something that is shared by you and your customer(s). We briefly mentioned joint project teams back in Chapter 5. This is where their value becomes even clearer.

10-Point Customer Focus Framework

#7. Joint Workouts

Most suppliers miss the opportunity to use their process improvement challenges as opportunities to engage, and stay engaged with, their customers. Most customers have some level of vested interest in your customer-facing processes being as effective as possible. And some customers will be willing to work with you to evaluate, plan, and implement steps that improve that effectiveness.

We're not suggesting you should ask for a customer's help in every process undertaking—not even in most of them. On a very selective basis, for those projects where it clearly makes sense, and the customer's potential gain is clear and meaningful, the idea of it becoming a joint project should not be dismissed outright. For every process improvement challenge you or your customers identify, your first internal question should be: is there a customer who can benefit from this such that they would team with you to work through it? Recall the GE-Sears and PPG examples. It can happen, and does happen—more often than you might think.

Value Chain Labs®—the Ultimate Dialogue

Before leaving Level II and starting the transition into Level III of the Customer Focus Maturity Model®, we want to mention one more technique that can come into play at Level II and help a supplier move into and sustain Level III. It's called a customer–supplier workout, and it actually is an extended and deeper form of joint project teaming. We first became aware of this unique and powerful form of cross-boundary engagement when GE used it. Soon after that, we experienced these workouts first-hand at Coopers & Lybrand (the firm subsequently merged in 1998 with Price Waterhouse to form PriceWaterhouseCoopers). There, learning under the external expertise of David Ulrich, who had worked directly with the GE workouts, we designed a client–provider (customer–supplier) workout initiative that would ultimately be conducted with several dozen of the firm's clients (customers).

We also studied similar cross-boundary processes used by such companies as PPG Industries, Motorola, General Reinsurance Corporation, and Ford Taurus. Based on that information and our prior experience, we developed Value Chain Labs® over 10 years ago to help companies break down the barriers between, and optimize the mutual gains of, their customer–supplier relationships.

Value Chain—Those entities and activities involved in the design, production, marketing, distribution, and support of an organization's products and services.

Lab—A place providing opportunity for analysis, discovery, and practice.

Value Chain Labs® is a carefully designed and closely facilitated workout process that brings a customer team and supplier team together to critically examine and improve their relationship with the ultimate goal being one of a mutually profitable and sustainable association. The issues the labs probe aren't always process-oriented issues. They might involve quality, costs, productivity, relationships, management systems, business systems, competitive threats, new product innovation, emerging markets, and myriad other issues or opportunities. They might be corrective discussions, fact-finding, or forward-looking discussions. The types of issues addressed by these workouts have covered the gamut of possibilities. The GE Appliance–Sears example earlier in this chapter was one of GE's early customer–supplier workouts. The global supplier (ABC Inc.) and their global energy customer discussed earlier was an example of a Value Chain Labs® workout.

The typical Lab takes approximately eight hours to conduct, although some have been longer, some have been shorter, and some have resulted in a series of subsequent Labs with other business units or functions in a particular customer–supplier connection. Three core elements make up the Value Chain Labs® workouts:

1. An innovative Business Case for Competitive Advantage. The business case creates a shared understanding and urgency around the need for a new, more profitable kind of customer–supplier relationship.

2. A proven method for constructively examining and addressing cross-boundary issues, concerns, and opportunities. This method redefines and becomes an ongoing part of the new, more sustainable, customer–supplier relationship.

3. An established change implementation model designed to close the gap between the relationship's current and desired state, as well as measure the progress of the relationship. This part ensures action takes place once the Lab is over.

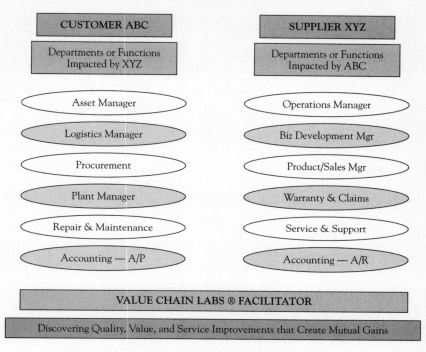

Figure 7.8 Lab Participants from Customer ABC and Supplier XYZ

The most effective Labs have been those with six to eight participants from the customer company and six to eight comparable participants from the supplier company, with those participants representing the key touch points in that particular relationship. We have had Labs with as few as 4 and 4 or as large as 12 and 12. An example of the participants from one of the more recent Value Chain Labs® is shown in Figure 7.8.

The above participants were part of a Lab that produced the following outcomes, among others:

For the Customer

- Identified roadblocks that were impeding progress and communications (internally and externally).

- Lowered procurement costs—less overhead and time through better focus upfront.
- Reduced operating costs since feature and function nuances and risks were built into product and service design.
- Positioned ABC to benefit early from new XYZ technologies, service enhancements, and resources.

For the Supplier

- Built customer loyalty and allowed XYZ to earn more ABC business through better performance.
- Improved resource utilization by redeploying resources to key value-creating processes and issues.
- Eliminated non-value-add activities to reduce operating costs and improve productivity.
- Aligned XYZ's approach and related key processes with ABC's business drivers.

Value Chain Labs® have been used successfully in dozens of different customer–supplier situations. Of those, generally speaking, 25 percent of the labs were for newly established relationships where the parties just wanted to ensure a successful launch or they had bad prior experiences and wanted to avoid a repeat in the new relationship. About 50 percent were for existing relationships where the parties wanted to take their partnering to the next level (i.e., usually moving from Level II to Level III), smooth out some rough spots, or become more consistent enterprise-wide. The other 25 percent were for at-risk situations where the customer was clearly unhappy, shopping competitive bids, or failing to renew a contract (most of these were at Level I).

We'll be discussing additional applications and outcomes from similar workout processes in later chapters. The key takeaway at this juncture, however, is to understand the powerful role joint workouts can play in creating engagement between customer personnel and supplier personnel, and directing that engagement around the review and improvement of mutually important processes. Once an organization develops some level of comfort and competency around the workout process, the next logical and natural extension is to use workouts to shape and drive the cultural adjustments and gains of Level III. While we present workouts here in our Level II discussion, they clearly are a tool that plays equally important roles at both Level II and Level III, which we'll discuss in Chapter 8.

Culture — The Soft Stuff *Is* the Hard Stuff

- Identify the four elements needed to realize Level III
- Create an internal language around value creation
- Use Ask, Act, and Align to shape your customer-focused culture

It's helpful to recap briefly before plunging into the steps and rewards of Level III. Without a solid grounding and progress at Levels I and II, achieving Level III won't likely be possible.

You'll remember the focus of Level II was to go beyond the transactions between customer and supplier, and look to better understand the reasons behind their behaviors in those transactions as well as the reasons for the related voice of the customer (VOC) measurement results. Whereas Level I activities were usually effective at detecting the customer's unmet needs, and recovering from or correcting the causes of not satisfying those needs, it was insufficient for understanding the customer's points of parity and points of differentiation that impacted their satisfaction throughout their total experience with the supplier. Level II efforts created reasons and opportunities to team with or engage the customer in an ongoing fashion so the supplier would have a more real-time view (instead of a rear-view mirror or snapshot) of what it takes to consistently satisfy the customer's myriad touch point owners. Only by consistently understanding and delivering on those various satisfaction drivers would the supplier earn the customer's trust and confidence needed to reveal their unstated needs. In effect, the customer is

Benefits of Teaming

- Turns VOC feedback and measures into actions.
- Engages and mobilizes much more than customer service and support teams.
- Turns touch points into points of dialogue and mutual support.
- Often reveals customer retention risks of which the supplier was unaware.
- Enhances the customer's awareness of the supplier's capabilities or solutions.
- Can result in substantive improvements in the way the supplier operates.
- Can result in substantive improvements in both sides' mutual processes.
- Starts building a sense of shared standards, ideas, and processes.
- Can set the stage for the partnering and leveraged culture Level III seeks.

saying: *Worry about getting the basics right first. Then, maybe we'll talk about ways we can do more business together!*

The ultimate goal of Level II, however, was to turn those multiple points of engagement into ongoing dialogues—dialogues that create opportunities to team and build mutually beneficial relationships. We saw that a supplier company with a Level II focus can enjoy several distinct benefits or advantages that impact its economic performance.

The Level II connections provide a far more complete picture of the customer's definition of value and many needs that the supplier would never have discovered in typical VOC activities. With that, a supplier is uniquely positioned to identify new solutions (offerings) for the customer, and improve existing offerings—all adding to the value the customer receives. That added value can then result in less price sensitivity, greater share of wallet (SOW), lower selling costs from repeat purchases, and additional revenue streams for the supplier. The improved processes associated with Level II can reduce cycle time and raise productivity for both sides, and lower the cost of ownership for the customer. And while all of that is taking place, the supplier is creating and strengthening its barriers to entry for the competition that further reduces selling costs, marketing expenses, and pricing pressure. Level II starts to create a fabric of loyalty that can be quite difficult for a competitor to break through. In sum—Level II has significant economic impact, and represents significant growth opportunity for the supplier.

Despite these clear and compelling benefits, there are some limitations to Level II that result in a supplier leaving significant economic and branding opportunities untapped. In addition, without embedding the customer focus such that it becomes part of and helps define the supplier's culture, the gains made at Level II, and even Level I, can backslide or unravel altogether. See Figure 8.1, which charts the Customer Focus Maturity Model® (CFMM) up to this point.

Level III moves past the *unmet* customer needs reported at Level I from rear-view looking voice-of-the-customer measures. It moves past

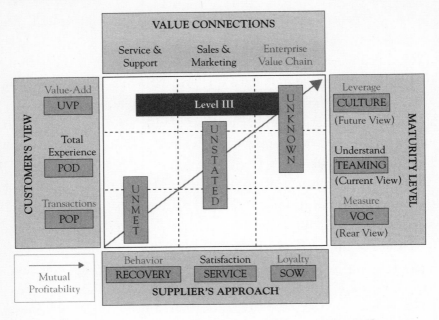

Figure 8.1   Customer Focus Maturity Model®

the deeper understanding of customer value and the *unstated* needs brought into view by Level II teaming activities. Level III creates a relationship where both sides jointly focus on the *unknown* possibilities and trends that might impact their respective and mutual businesses further down the road (future view). It seeks to build on the VOC and teaming practices of the first two levels, and embed those practices into the culture on both sides of the customer–supplier relationship. Level III creates a customer-centric culture that is leveraged across the entire supplier organization—aligning the self-centered silos, protected turfs, and competing agendas that can stall or dismantle customer focus progress. Level III establishes customer value as the common fiber linking all of the supplier's philosophies, objectives, processes, and practices. Level III also provides the model, evidence, venues, and tools to encourage a corresponding or reciprocal focus throughout the customer organization, and eventually throughout other parts of the supplier's value chain. Sound ambitious? You bet it is! Ambitious and achievable.

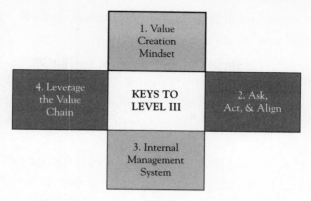

Figure 8.2   Key Elements of Level III

Four distinct, but interrelated, key elements are involved in achieving Level III, as shown in Figure 8.2.

1. Develop an internal *Value Creation Mindset*, awareness and language
2. Build the *Ask, Act, and Align* approach into everything you do
3. Create the *Internal Management System* for sustaining a customer-centric culture
4. Leverage the mindset, approach, and system throughout the *Value Chain*

Key Element 1: Develop a Value Creation Mindset

This first element goes back to something we explained in our process orientation discussion in Chapter 7. The sole reason a company—your company, any company—exists is to create economic value for its various stakeholders. And no stakeholder will realize any value unless and until the customer does. To generate value for any stakeholder, your company must first generate value for its customer.

When we ask people to describe their business to us, we almost always get an answer that revolves around that company's products or services or industry. Rarely will the answer include the notion that the company exists to create customer value or to serve some customer. The cold truth is—at the end of the day—if you don't create something unique and valuable for your customer, nothing else will matter. It's not your products and services that pay your bills; it's the customer's purchase of those products and services that pays your bills.

Simply put, your entire organization exists for the sole purpose of identifying, creating, and delivering customer value. Your company is part of a value chain. More specifically, it's a link in that value chain that forms a connection between your suppliers and your customers.

So the first key to reaching Level III is to begin changing how your employees and managers perceive the purpose of the company. This entails being very clear about why your company exists and the broader value chain within which it exists.

Once this view of the company's external role has been established, a similar context and language must be created for the company's internal roles. When we ask managers and employees in a given company to describe how the company is made up or structured, the answer we usually get is in terms of an organization chart. That is, most people describe the company's make-up in terms of business units, departments, functions, roles, or responsibilities.

In reality, any company is made up of a series of processes that are linked together to create customer value (i.e., to fill the customers' needs). When a business unit, department, or function identifies its role or purpose, it should be defined in the broader terms of how the function contributes to the value creation process. Whether it's accounting, engineering, production, procurement, customer service, human resources, sales, marketing, or any myriad other functions—each has a role to play in the process of creating and delivering customer value.

For example, at Walt Disney World there are 2,000 job descriptions, but there is only one purpose of every single one of those jobs: *to create satisfied customers.*[1] Another example is the phrase Southwest Airlines puts at the bottom of every paycheck: "This paycheck is made possible because of your customers."[2] The more an organization defines, emphasizes, and talks about that broader, overarching customer process and the roles within it, the more employees and managers begin looking at the larger picture.

One of the problems we typically encounter in this value chain discussion is the tendency many companies have to use terms like "external customers" and "internal customers." There is only one customer—the person or company who buys the products or services your company sells. Everyone in your company must see himself or herself, not as part of a particular department or business unit, but first and foremost as part of an end-to-end process that exists for the common purpose of generating customer value.

When people in the organization have to think about internal versus external customers, it can cause confusion, cynicism, division, and misalignment of purpose. Winning companies define, organize, and manage themselves around the customer's experience. And to do that effectively, there can only be one definition of "customer."

People need one true north that whenever there's a decision to be made—there's no question about which customer the decision must benefit. Every employee, from the lowest skilled or paid to the highest, needs to think, act, and talk like there is only one kind of customer. That's the kind of focused, single-purposed, aligned mindset companies need if they wish to reap the gains of Level III.

As straightforward as this might seem, it has proved challenging for many organizations. Your people have been conditioned to think of and identify with their job, function, or department. Seeing

---

[1] Rob Morton, "Disney Institute Case Study–Humana." Retrieved from www.trainingindustry.com.
[2] Lorraine Grubbs-West, *Lessons In Loyalty: How Southwest Airlines Does It—An Insider's View* (Dallas, TX: CornerStone Leadership Institute, 2005), 111.

themselves as part of the broader company, or a customer-value-creation process, is not natural for them. It will be uncomfortable for some, counterintuitive for others, and downright contentious for others. This new way of thinking, behaving, and operating is a significant mind-shift, so repetition will be critical for the unlearning, and learning—needed to succeed.

Key Element 2: Ask, Act, and Align Everything You Do

Level III requires another key element that involves three actions (you may want to remember them as the triple "A's"): *ask, act*, and *align*. Figures 8.3, 8.4, and 8.5 highlight each one, respectively.

Asking Questions Is an Obligation

In a customer-centric culture, or any high-performance culture, every employee has permission and an obligation to ask the tough questions. This is important to a company's customer focus for at least three reasons:

1. People need to ensure they have the clarity they need to proceed—clarity around where they're going as well as why there, why them, and why now. They must ask questions to ensure they have that clarity. Without it, they create their own direction, priorities, and responsibilities.

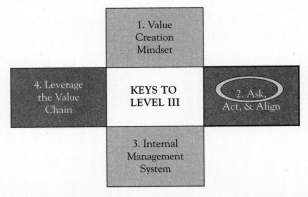

Figure 8.3   Always Ask the Important Questions

Strategies may be conceived in the executive offices, but they are implemented on the front lines where employees come into daily contact with products, services, customers, and suppliers. The strategy or plan might be crystal clear to those who developed it, but it needs to be equally clear to those who must carry it out.

That clarity can't be achieved just by using a top-down communications process. The message needs to be accurately heard, processed, and translated into action and results. Then the impact of those actions, as well as any unplanned results and new developments, need to be fed back up the chain of command for continual evaluation and response. Leaders need real-time, unfiltered access to what's happening in the trenches. This requires an effective bottom-up communications process in addition to a top-down process. For a culture that executes consistently, employees must continually ask questions of their leaders and feed relevant information to them.

For example, Harley-Davidson made intellectual curiosity one of its five core values. As former chairman Richard Teerlink explained: "All employees must be willing to question why things are being done the way they are. Open-minded review of every aspect of an organization is essential for success."[3]

2. Encourage your employees to think about how various ideas, policies, and decisions might affect the customer's experience. For example, a sales manager at Siemens AG often carried a folding chair with him into internal meetings. Whenever someone would ask what the chair was for, the manager's answer was, "This is my customer's chair. I brought it into the meeting so my customer can sit right here and listen to our discussion." After a while, people got used to the fact that the

---

[3] Ron Ashkenas et al., *The Boundaryless Organization: Breaking the Chains of Organizational Structure*, rev. ed. (San Francisco: Jossey-Bass, 2002), 170.

customer was a key stakeholder and a core consideration in their ongoing plans and decisions, and reminded everyone to ask—what would our customer say? How would our customer react?[4]

In another company, the CEO was intense and relentless in monthly staff meetings when it came to discussing financial and operating results. A core part of each meeting was a discussion about how the company's products, services, and practices were affecting the customer's experience. Some specific questions the CEO often asked included the following:

How does that or will that make our customers' lives easier?

How will that impact the customers' total cost of owning our product?

How will that increase the customers' yield on their production lines?

At Harley Davidson, a truly exceptional brand and success story, the management team is continually challenged to answer three questions:

1. What have we learned (from that situation)?

2. What will be the impact on our people (and various stakeholders)?

3. How can we get everyone involved and excited (about it)?[5]

If every employee either directly or indirectly impacts the customer's experience with your company, then every employee has the right, and obligation, to advocate for that customer.

There are just too many competitors thinking about ways to displace you, and too many opportunities for a company to

[4] Don Peppers and Martha Rogers, *Rules to Break and Laws to Follow: How Your Business Can Beat the Crisis of Short-Termism*, (John Wiley & Sons, Inc., 2008).
[5] Ron Ashkenas et al., *The Boundaryless Organization: Breaking the Chains of Organizational Structure*, (San Francisco: Jossey-Bass, 1995), 68.

underperform in the customer's eyes and let a competitor in. Every employee in your company, not just the CEO or customer experience officer (CXO), must be charged with asking questions that ensure you are staying focused on the customer and considering all possibilities.

This responsibility to ask goes beyond the department or functional area of the employee. An accountant in the finance department should feel encouraged to raise questions about product quality just as much as a sales person should feel empowered to challenge the way an invoice was handled by the billing department. A customer service rep should feel permitted to challenge an account rep who over-promised something to a customer, and the account rep should be expected to confront the transportation manager who failed to let the account rep know a customer delivery had been significantly delayed.

In effect, creating a customer experience that differentiates your company in the marketplace requires everybody in your company to take off their blinders. If an employee sees, hears, or suspects a decision or behavior that might cause customer problems, that employee must know he or she has permission— an obligation—to call each other out on the issue no matter what department the employee is in. So the second role "ask" plays is that everyone has the right to ask tough questions of each other—even across the silos—if it means improving the customer's experience.

3. Ask customers what they think, what they like, what they don't like, and so forth. We talked at length about this when we discussed VOC, but we want to reinforce a few other aspects here. You need to continually ask customers for their input—looking back at recent experiences and looking forward to future needs. Too often, companies think they know what customers want and how well the company is doing at meeting those wants, only to find that those views are not what the customer thinks at all.

Here's a way to test understanding of the customer's point of view in your own company the next time you have a group of employees together. It's most effective in Level II when you're trying to generate a broader base of employee awareness and support. Assuming you have gathered the employees in a meeting room, you'll want to choose two opposing walls of the room for this exercise. Let's call them the north wall and the south wall. Put a piece of paper on the far left end of the north wall and write the word "worst" on it. Put another piece of paper on the far right end of the same north wall and write the word "best" on it. Do the exact same thing on the opposing south wall with two fresh pieces of paper—one with the word "worst" and one with the word "best" written on it.

Now pull half of the employees aside and privately ask them to think about how well they think the company is doing at providing its customers with a quality experience. Ask them to stand against the north wall—picking a position anywhere between the two pieces of paper that represents their individual answers or views. Ask them to remain standing in their chosen positions until instructed to return to their seats. Note where they all stand, how dispersed or clustered they are, and how many are at the best end versus the worst end versus the middle.

With the first group still standing along the north wall, privately ask the other half of employees to put themselves in the customers' shoes and think honestly about how the customers view the quality of the experience they're having with your company. Have them stand against the opposite south wall— once again picking a position anywhere between the two pieces of paper that represents their individual answers. Note where they stand and how it compares to the first group. You can then ask each group to describe what they were asked to represent along their respective walls, and have them explain why they took the positions they did. Most of the times we do this exercise, it shows rather quickly how internal and external views can differ about the quality of your customer's experience.

The point is, you can't assume you know what the customer is feeling, thinking, or wanting on a real-time basis. In different ways, and at different touch points, you continually have to ask.

Building a culture where people are encouraged, comfortable enough, and obligated to ask tough questions is critical to a successful customer focus. You need a company-wide expectation that everyone, regardless of level and function, asks tough questions that help the company learn and improve the customer's experience—questions of their leaders, of each other, of their suppliers, and of the customer.

The FUD Factor

When a company starts taking a deeper, more rigorous, often more painful look at their customer focus strengths and weaknesses, it's common for the FUD factor to start creeping in. And the further a company gets into Level II activities and starts asking more questions about how it operates, the more exposed it feels—oftentimes causing a reluctance to move into Level III.

The FUD factor oftentimes (and ironically) causes a reluctance to move into Level III, the very thing that can enhance your customer–supplier connection. The more you learn about your customer's world, and your ability or inability to impact that world, the more squeamish your managers and customer-facing employees might become. It's quite common for the naysayers and cynics in your organization to start raising concerns and offering resistance as you move further along the customer focus journey. The source of that resistance is often:

(continued)

- *Fear* about the customer bringing up old issues, or new issues that you haven't resolved or didn't even know about.

- *Uncertainty* about the organization's ability to resolve certain issues to the customer's satisfaction or to make the types of institutional or cultural changes needed to create a consistently exceptional customer experience.

- *Doubt* about the company's resolve or true commitment to this effort and willingness to make tough decisions or take a stand—both internally and externally.

In terms of *fear* about what customers might say, the reality is that you can't fight the enemy you can't see. Just because you don't ask for a customer's input or ask how satisfied they are, doesn't mean they aren't harboring negative feelings about you or aren't looking for ways to replace you as their supplier. And if they are harboring ill feelings about you, whether or not they are admitting it to you, you can bet they are telling others about it—including other potential customers of yours. It's true that asking their opinion could expose your company to other problems you didn't know about, but wouldn't you rather have that out in the open than working invisibly against you?

The *uncertainty* about your ability to resolve an issue is something most companies give more time and attention to than it deserves. When it comes to soliciting and responding to customer feedback, there are a couple of realities that we mentioned earlier but bear repeating as many don't consider them, or they lose sight of them:

- Many problems customers raise are of the low-hanging fruit variety where the solution is not that difficult; and where something can't be reversed or recovered, it can be avoided in the future.

- Saying "no" to a customer request is not inherently bad—as long as you do it in a way that furthers the relationship, instead of frustrating it.
- Lastly, the customer is not always right and not all customer requests or complaints are yours to fix—sometimes the customer is the problem and they own the remedy.

The *doubt* factor typically revolves around the supplier company's resolve or true commitment to the customer focus. It is the most challenging aspect of the FUD factor. To combat doubt, the senior leadership team must operate as an aligned, customer-focused, persistent, and highly engaged team. This is where senior leadership turns their customer focus into either an initiative du jour, or an initiative that endures. We'll be discussing the need for ways to achieve leadership commitment shortly.

Your most unhappy customers are your greatest source of learning.
—Bill Gates, Microsoft

Acting on What You Learn

The next key is to act on the information you get when you ask questions. (See Figure 8.4.)

We have seen far too many VOC initiatives, and even internal survey processes, that ask for input and then don't really do anything with the input they get. In most cases, asking and not acting is worse than not having asked at all. The main purpose of asking tough questions is to learn and improve from the answers. A customer-focused culture is also a learning culture.

A great example of this occurred in the 2008 Summer Olympic Games in Beijing. Following the final round and closing ceremonies of the men's court volleyball competition, the gold-medal-winning USA team's coach Hugh McCutcheon said that no one gave this

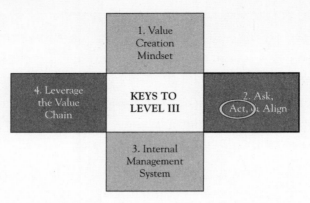

Figure 8.4   Always Act on Answers

team a prayer last year of doing well in these games—much less winning the gold. They hadn't won gold in 20 years. The team, however, proved everyone wrong by beating Brazil in the final round. When a reporter asked McCutcheon what he felt the key was to this team's success, he said, "It was their ability to learn. They took each game one at a time, learned from it, and applied those learnings to the next one. They truly *learned* how to win."

Learning doesn't happen just by asking. It happens by first asking, then acting. You then apply it to new situations, ask some more, learn some more, and apply it further. To succeed, a customer-focused culture must have a penchant for both learning and action. You can't get bogged down in gathering and/or analyzing input or data. You need to develop as comprehensive a view as possible, as quickly as you possibly can, and start acting on it. You can always fine-tune and adjust as you go based on new data or further analyses.

Winning organizations are those who move faster, communicate clearly, and involve everyone in a focused effort to serve a more demanding customer.

—*Jack Welch, GE*

We see too many companies over-engineer the learning process such that they are forever reviewing something and never get to the doing something. And by the time the company acts, the nature of the problem has changed, the problem has gone away altogether (which isn't always a good outcome) or somebody else has already solved it. "Ask and act" is a two-punch combination that keeps your customer in front of you and focused on you, and keeps your opponents on the outside looking in.

Take for example, one specialty manufacturing company that had just finished conducting their second annual customer satisfaction survey. The survey was made up of 15 individually scored questions and two open-ended questions. The prior year's survey was generally good, with a 42 percent response rate and an overall average satisfaction score of 4.25 out of a possible perfect score of 5.0.

The company spent the better part of a month going over the detailed survey results to identify anything they considered urgent or really problematic, but nothing stood out. Not quite sure how or whether to do anything with the findings, they put the survey on the back burner for the time being.

Two months later, one of their customers called to inquire about something unrelated, and just in passing before hanging up, asked how the survey process had gone. This inquiry, though isolated, got the company thinking once more about what to do with the survey results. But given that a couple months had now passed, the thought was that there really wasn't anything in the results screaming for action, and given that they only knew of one customer who showed any interest in the status of the survey, the survey follow-up was placed on the back burner once again.

The next year's survey results for the same set of respondents were noticeably different. This time they had a 57 percent response rate and an overall average satisfaction score of 3.85 out of a possible perfect 5.0. There was a decline from their prior year's scores in 13 of the 15 questions, and several of the individual question scores were below 2.0. Moreover, the prior year's survey resulted in some 40 written responses to the open-ended questions, but this year's results reflected over 200 written responses—the majority of which were neutral or negative. Overall, this was a decidedly different picture for the company.

Obviously, the company needed to quickly understand what was driving this year's significantly lower results. Fortunately for this particular manufacturing company, it didn't take long to figure it out. The written comments made it clear that in addition to some reported problems driving the second year's lower ratings, the customers didn't appreciate not hearing anything back from last year's survey efforts. Several went further to urge the company to not bother them again as this was clearly a waste of time on both sides. The survey questions with scores showing the most significant year-over-year declines were the questions dealing with communications, follow-through, and commitment to quality service. Clearly, their inaction in the prior year had left an impression on their customers—and it wasn't a good one.

Another fortunate factor for this company was that this year they were ready with a post-survey action plan. They quickly compiled and evaluated the results, and within three weeks had a follow-up communication going out to all customers whether they responded to the survey or not. Obviously, that communication wasn't conclusive and didn't announce any wholesale changes or solutions, but it did highlight the key findings from the survey, set forth a timeline for further examining and responding to those key findings, and had an appropriate amount of humility and apology for the prior year's inaction.

The key lessons one can learn from this company's experience include the following:

- If you don't plan to act—don't ask.
- You don't need to be 100 percent ready before acting.
- Don't underestimate the value of small action steps.
- At a minimum, tell customers a few key areas you're further evaluating or analyzing.

- Tell customers how soon they can expect an update or action.
- Acting includes acknowledging things you can't address in the short term.
- Acting includes telling customers things you might not ever be able to address.
- Create follow-up expectations that you can meet.
- Say what you'll do by when—then make sure you do.

For years, we have seen companies learn the hard way about not acting soon enough, not acting substantively enough or not acting at all. Companies that have relied on these six standards of VOC action have fared much better.

The Six Standards of VOC Action

1. Get the customer's feedback and thank them for it.
2. Tell them something as soon as you can (don't wait for 100 percent complete plans).
3. Tell them what you can't do and why.
4. Tell them what you will do and by when.
5. Give them periodic, concise updates with contacts that can provide more detail.
6. Remind them: you asked, they replied, you acted, and they benefited.

Another important characteristic of the learning culture that's so important to a supplier's customer focus is to foster what we call a "no-blame zone." We find that when people are given clear expectations and goals, and the parameters of their ability to make decisions and take risks, they tend to make far more good decisions than bad ones. And the bad ones they do make tend to be moderate to minimal in their impact.

For example, we worked with one particular organization that had been struggling to establish a meaningful, actionable vision and value statement. After a series of discussions with them, we proposed what they referred to as the company's core value statement. Surprisingly, it wasn't what you would normally think when you hear that often over-spoken and under-used term—*core values*. For this company, which we'll call AB Co, that term would take on a slightly different meaning. In effect, their core value statement provided that no one could ever go wrong, be questioned, be criticized or "blamed," if they acted or made a decision based on the company's three values:

1. We value safety above all else—the safe way will always be the right way.
2. We do all we can to create value for our customers—provided it's safe.
3. We do all we can to build AB Co's economic value—provided it serves our customers.

The proposed core value statement went on to explain that anyone who feels they can't support and help advance these three values probably wouldn't like working here and probably won't succeed working here. Of course the real key is how they implement and enforce their three values. But everyone was struck by the clarity of it and how it distilled the organization's essence into something that provided simple and clear guidance.

Some companies, however, are not at all forgiving when it comes to its people making mistakes. Instead of focusing on finding the root cause, and letting everyone learn and grow from it, they focus on finding the guilty party, which causes everyone to cover up or run from it.

For a customer focus to succeed, people need to feel comfortable about making thoughtful decisions and acting in the absence of complete information, without fear of punishment. Obviously, repeating one's mistakes is not learning and that's not what we're condoning here. But few things will derail a customer focus faster than a blaming environment. Especially when it's obvious enough for the customer to pick up on it. The enemy is the competition— the enemy is out there. You can't afford to be taking pot shots at your employees as they learn and improve—get the guns aiming outside, at the real enemy.

Something else we mentioned earlier bears repeating here. Remember that customer focus is a process, and as such, it never ends. Hand in hand with that notion is the importance of continuous improvement. As long as your customers' businesses, markets, and needs change, your ability to create value for them will have to change as well. To sustain a customer focus, a supplier has to have a commitment to continuous learning and improvement. That means the ask and act approach has to become a way of life—part of the culture.

There's one parting comment we need to make before leaving this section about acting. In addition to requiring a learning culture, customer focus also requires a culture of execution (i.e., acting on your plan). Too many organizations dive into some aspect of a customer focus effort thinking it's going to rescue them from their operational or execution problems. The fact is, a company that struggles with execution in general, is similarly going to struggle with implementing a customer focus. Focusing on the customer won't in and of itself "fix" a company that has ineffective management practices. We'll say a bit more about that shortly.

Build Alignment Across Your Company

As we've noted before, customer focus can't be viewed as the responsibility of one department, but must be viewed as everyone's responsibility. It's not enough for just one or two departments to be good at asking and acting; the entire organization must be

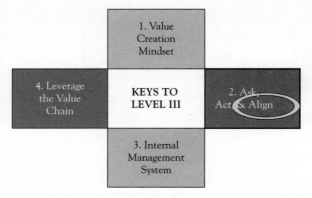

Figure 8.5   Align Your Value-Creation Efforts

aligned around this model and its emphasis on value creation. (See Figure 8.5.)

Alignment has two dimensions to it when it comes to your customer focus. The first, internal alignment, is to create an alignment of purpose, process, measures, and accountabilities throughout your organization—across all functions and at all levels. The second, external alignment, is to build that same alignment across your value chain. We'll delve into internal alignment here, and cover external alignment later in Chapter 10.

When we talk about internal alignment, there are several ideas we're striving to make real. One that we've already discussed is the idea that there can only be one definition of "customer" in your organization—and that is the customer who buys your products and services.

> *There is only one boss. The customer. And he can fire everybody in the company from the chairman on down, simply by spending his money somewhere else.*
>
> —*Sam Walton*

Another aspect of internal alignment is to ensure all employees realize that the reason you exist, and the reason their jobs exist, is to create value for the customer. Earlier we talked about empowering

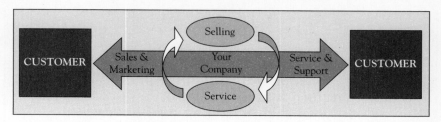

Figure 8.6   Sales and Service: Mindsets in Customer Focus

and expecting every employee to ask the tough questions when he or she sees or hears something that might create a customer experience problem or opportunity.

In effect, you need every employee, regardless of title, to see sales *and* service as part of *his or her* job. (See Figure 8.6.) Sales and service are mindsets as much as they are departments. Every employee must be able to represent (sell/market) your company in a favorable light, and every employee must be alert for ways to support your customer focus efforts (serve/support).

In essence, you want every employee being an advocate or ambassador for your company and brand promise, and you want every employee looking for and seizing opportunities to deliver on that promise. We really appreciated the reaction from the CEO of one company when we explained the above concept to him and his executive team. As he explained: *No one is so high up on the organization chart that they can't pick up a piece of paper on the floor or answer a ringing phone in the lobby. And no one is so far down on the organization chart that they shouldn't be able to describe how we help our customers.* Well said!

Still another aspect of internal alignment is to help every employee understand the way your company makes money, the impact the customer has on that money-making process, and the many ways the customer experiences or is touched by your company in that process. This, too, we discussed in earlier chapters, but here's an example that illustrates several of these points.

An Aligned Mindset at W.W. Grainger, Inc.

Desperate to buy steel-tipped boots in order to gain access to an active construction site—or lose a day's wages for not having safe-enough shoes—a man walked into a W.W. Grainger store in Lawrence, Massachusetts, only to find that the location did not have his size in stock.

Although Grainger, a Lake Forest, Illinois–based business-to-business supplier of more than 500,000 products, could supply the boots the following day, that wasn't going to solve the construction worker's problem. Just then, a Grainger employee realized he was the same size and offered up his own pair of boots.

"That customer could not believe it," says Kim Cysewski, a vice president of HR at Grainger. "We empower our team members to go above and beyond like that to keep our customers satisfied. Employees understand the connection [between] doing more business, improving the business results, and their personal contribution to that."

Jared Shelley, "Time to Re-Engage," *Human Resource Executive* online

(December 1, 2010, www.hreonline.com/HRE/story.jsp?storyId=533326217&query=Grainger)

The connection Grainger wants and helps its employees to make—the connection that links customer satisfaction, company success, and personal contribution—is the exact mindset sought by customer-focused organizations. It's a consistent understanding—a persistent view—that permeates the entire organization.

Unfortunately, some senior leaders view "mindset" or "alignment" as consultant babble or some soft, intangible term that everyone talks about but no one can really demonstrate. To those leaders, we ask: *Would you be willing to let your customers wander through your company's halls or facilities, unescorted, talking to any employee they wish about anything they wish?* Probably not! The reason you wouldn't take that chance is that you aren't sure about or comfortable with the things the customer might see or hear. You lack that certainty and comfort because you know there isn't a unified or shared focus on the customer within your organization—at least not at the shop floor or cubicle level. Call it whatever you want, but you know when you lack it. We call it alignment, and while it might be difficult to describe or grasp, it's fairly obvious when it's missing. It's equally obvious when it exists in any organization.

A great example of alignment can be found at Harley-Davidson with something they call "Freedom with Fences." That's their approach to employee involvement and engagement. They want their workers suggesting improvements and making decisions within reasonable parameters (i.e., fences).

They have flattened the organization so those closest to the action have the responsibility, and authority, to get things done. Their management organization chart is made up of three overlapping circles: Create Demand (Sales and Marketing); Produce Products (Engineering and Manufacturing); and the Support Circle (Legal, Financial, HR, and Communications). The circles nominate nine people to their Leadership and Strategy Council, the group that looks at issues cutting across all three circles.[6]

Ask employees about their views on working for Harley Davidson. They won't recite the Harley credo or talk about core values. Instead, they mention the importance of the "team," and the pride they feel in their work. As one fellow put it—"I don't own a bike, but there are five Harley owners who live in my neighborhood. Everyone knows where I work. When your neighbors use and talk about the bikes you make, you can't help but pay attention to

---

[6] Gina Imperato, "Harley Shifts Gears," *Fast Company* 9 (June/July 1997): 104.

your job. And I expect the rest of these guys (the crew) to do the same. Anything else is unacceptable."[7]

That's alignment! There's not a potential customer, potential investor, or prospective employee who you wouldn't want to hear that message if it were coming from one of *your* people about *your* company! We said earlier that while strategies are conceived at the executive level, they are achieved (or not) at the entry level. No matter how committed a senior leader genuinely is to the customer focus, or how committed they appear to be, the employees are the ones whose commitment matters the most. They can touch and impact far more customers and potential customers than any senior leader can. That's what makes this Level III culture so important to optimizing and sustaining the benefits of a successful customer focus.

Someone once said that your company's culture is what your people do when you're not around. In our view, compliance is what they do when you *are* around. A customer-focused culture is created by your employees' beliefs and actions even when you're not around. The more aligned those beliefs and actions are, the more consistent your customer focus will be. Which would you rather have—compliance with your customer focus, or a culture that embodies it?

To achieve the kind of end-to-end consistency typical of Level III companies, you need to have internal alignment around three key principles:

1. There is only one type of customer—the external one.
2. That customer is the reason your company, and the jobs within it, exist.
3. Employee beliefs and actions must reinforce the above two ideas.

---

[7] Kansas City Harley-Davidson plant tour and meetings with work teams; May 2003 in conjunction with the annual Customer-Supplier Division Conference for the American Society of Quality.

We've spent some time in this chapter emphasizing the importance, impact, and examples of a customer-focused culture. What we haven't yet discussed is how to go about building such a culture or mindset. In the next chapter, we turn to that with a detailed look at the internal management system needed to make this all happen and continue happening.

CHAPTER 9

Managing Change, Performance, and Talent

- Identify your capacity for customer-centric change and the three levels of change companies must manage
- Apply the peak performance model to drive and support your customer focus journey
- Leverage your talent management pivot points to advance your customer focus

In the last chapter, we introduced the four elements of a Level III customer focus (Figure 9.1). We also went into detail on the first two of those elements—develop a *value creation mindset* and take an *ask, act, and align approach (the triple "A's")*. In this chapter, we'll move into the third element or step, which is ensuring that your *internal management system* supports and drives your customer focus.

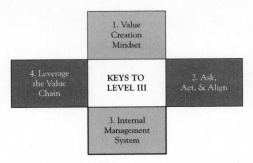

Figure 9.1   Level III—Internal Management System

Key Element 3: Apply An Effective Internal Management System

The management system we are referring to isn't a system in the technological sense, but a series of management practices and tools that are integrated with the customer focus and work in concert with each other.

This section is not meant to be a comprehensive or exhaustive view of an entire management system, which would include operating, financial, and other management processes. Rather, it deals with the three management areas—*change management*, *performance management*, and *talent management*—that are most vital to an effective customer focus journey.

As part of this discussion, we'll also highlight the remaining three elements of our 10-Point Customer Focus Framework: *capacity for change*, *consequences*, and *committed leadership*.

As was the case in some of our earlier discussions, there is a fair amount of overlap and connection between these various management areas and framework elements. As a result, our discussion about them will be more woven than linear. Figure 9.2 loosely depicts the relationships between these various pieces and will serve as a general guide to our discussion.

We begin by looking at the role change plays in a supplier's customer focus. By its very nature, a customer focus journey is about a process—a process of continual discovery, improvement, and growth. In every respect, it's a process of change.

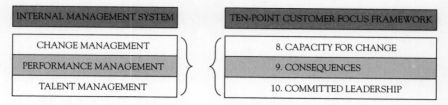

Figure 9.2   Your Internal Management System Drives Your Customer Focus

Key Change Management Practices

There are several common tools or levers that suppliers use to drive and support their customer-driven change process. They include, but are not limited to: clearly and consistently defining their customer focus; measuring and reminding people about the company's progress; deploying and showcasing change champions; and maintaining persistent, relevant, internal communications. Two other vital tools or levers involve consequences and committed leadership. We will discuss these later.

The first important step is to define your customer focus in clear, easy-to-remember and easy-to-explain terms. You must use realistic everyday terms, not the hyperbolic, exotic terms typical of many mission and vision statements. Remember our earlier discussions in Chapter 6 about employee engagement and readiness? Your employees must be able to translate your customer focus at a very individual level so they can readily describe it to others and clearly understand the role they play in it. This means that all of your communications cannot be designed for the management reader—they must, more importantly, be designed for the shop floor and office cubicle reader. In addition, you must ensure that definition and purpose are always visible. This must be active, not passive, visibility. We don't mean keeping your customer focus someplace where everyone has access to it. We mean keeping it someplace where people can't avoid seeing it.

The second key change management tool is to set and measure realistic expectations for results or progress. Pick the top 3 to 5 key customer focus metrics you want to measure. Then set short-term, mid-term, and longer-term goals for those metrics, and maniacally communicate the status of them. Many organizations make progress against their customer focus goals—whether quantitative or qualitative goals—a topic of every staff meeting, just like financial results, production, safety, or other key objectives and results. Others show it as the first regular topic in a regularly distributed company newsletter, or as a daily or weekly update on computer splash screens, intranet log-in pages, paycheck stuffers, and so on. We don't just mean posting the numerical results or statistics in a cold, uninspiring fashion like that of most financial and operating reports. We mean surrounding them with a brief illustrative message or a recent success story (recall Ritz-Carlton's wow stories in Chapter 6) so you can celebrate, compliment, and thank people for their specific roles in generating the progress or results.

The third change management tool or lever is to identify and engage, as soon as possible, your team of internal change champions. We referred to this concept earlier in Chapter 6. Get these informal leaders to provide staff meeting updates, lead related projects or initiatives, and serve as a conduit between the other employees in their department or assigned area and the customer focus leader(s) or senior management team. Equally important is to publicly recognize, showcase, and commend these champions on the roles they're playing. Make it clear to everyone that this is the behavior and support you expect and are happy to reward. Show your organization that these are the role models you hope everyone aspires to emulate.

One other area inferred in the above points, but which needs to be highlighted, is internal communications. One aspect of such communications is general sharing of customer-focus–related information. The organization needs a systematic process that shares—enterprise-wide—the lessons, actions, and new processes, policies, or tools that come out of your customer focus efforts. This is particularly important where a supplier is significantly involved in Level II teaming activities—with its many moving parts and projects. We see many situations where a particular business unit, product line, or functional area has discovered a customer-impacting issue or has created a solution to one, and the rest of the company doesn't know about it.

Another related problem is one we frequently see occur in multiple-product or service-line companies. In these cases, a special allowance or problem fix provided to a customer by one product line in the supplier company was denied that same customer by another product line in that same supplier company. We're not suggesting there might not be a perfectly valid reason for the dual treatment, but oftentimes there is no valid reason. The reason was miscommunication within the supplier organization. These communication breakdowns can cause costly duplicated effort, lost time, internal feelings of mismanagement, and external perceptions of a disconnected organization.

Internal communications must be persistent. Your customer focus communications need to be provided regularly—almost obsessively. We say this because people learn through repetition, and that's important to a customer focus in at least two ways. First, people need to know that this focus is not an initiative du jour, and is not going to fade away. It's a persistent, enduring focus that they cannot outlast. One way to help them see that is to never let up on your communication, which means continuous reinforcement of your core messages, your priorities, and results. Repetition is also important because a customer focus usually entails as much *unlearning* as it does *new learning*. Employees often need help clearing their minds of old models and philosophies as well as old approaches and priorities. Repetition helps them unlearn so they can learn the improved ways of doing the things you'll need them to do throughout the customer focus journey.

One final aspect of an organization's communications practices relates to creating some internal momentum and branding for your customer focus. Companies miss substantial opportunities to advance their customer focus effort by not helping people connect the dots between various improvements in the organization and the organization's customer focus. Whenever a policy, process, practice, system, or tool is improved, there's a real good chance that improvement can be traced back to something learned or discovered from a customer. You need to help people see that linkage at every possible turn. We talked earlier in our voice-of-the-customer discussion about the importance of continually reminding your customers that: *you asked, they responded, you acted, and they benefitted.* Similarly, in your internal management system, you need to continually remind your employees of how various changes are driven by or connected to the customer's experience. In effect, you're saying to them: *our customers asked and we're responding.* Even better is to say: *we asked, they responded, we acted, and both sides benefitted.* The overarching message here is that we don't change just for the sake of changing. We change for the sake of our customer's experience. The more you remind them of that, the more embedded it becomes in their way of thinking.

One small but perfect example of something companies do to short-circuit their change efforts is that they constantly revise their internal policies and procedures. We discovered the hidden impact of this seemingly harmless practice when we were interviewing managers and supervisors at one particular organization, and it had surprising customer focus implications. We learned that an average of at least two policy revisions per month went out to the organization's managers and supervisors. We sensed that was too much so we started asking about it. We were right. The managers and supervisors had gotten to the point of not even reading the revisions, and just putting them in the policy manual binder, or letting them pile up on their desk or credenza, or even throwing them away. There clearly was a cynicism about the value of the policy manual and consequently the credibility of the organization's senior leaders.

In general, because the updates were so difficult to keep track of and stay apprised of, the organization got to the point where they simply ignored updates. In time, they stopped relying on the manual entirely—because they knew they hadn't kept it up to date. Instead of referring to it as a management tool, they would go to each other, or to someone in administration, for the answer. We discussed this with the CEO and expressed our concern that it was not only chewing up productive time, but it was diluting her credibility even though she wasn't the source of the constant stream of revisions.

We suggested an "über policy"—one that governs all the other policies. That über policy stated: there can be no more changes to the internal policies and procedures manual unless it is required by law or required by your customers. What we were suggesting, in effect, is if it doesn't improve the customer's experience, don't change it. Obviously, there would be exceptions periodically, but constant revisions would no longer be the norm. There are two key takeaways from this particular organization's example. One, be careful using change as an excuse for making frequent, annoying policy and procedure revisions that aren't business-driven. They can cause numbness throughout the organization that will impair your more substantive and mission-critical change efforts. Two, try to get into the habit of connecting your changes to your customer focus. Where you do change something, it's to your advantage to help everyone understand how the change was driven by or related to the customer's experience.

10-Point Customer Focus Framework

#8. Capacity for Change

Every customer-focused company, regardless of where they are on the Customer Focus Maturity Model® (CFMM), will require some degree of change at various points of their journey. One of the misconceptions people have, however, is thinking a customer focus requires a new or different culture for the organization. That's rarely the case in our experience. Organizations need to understand those aspects of their culture that still create or add value, and then work hard to preserve and leverage them. Conversely, though, organizations need to be honest about identifying and pruning philosophies, policies, and practices that do not create or add value. The question is not *which culture do you prefer—the current one or a different one?* The question is *which current aspects do you keep, which ones do you let go of, and which new ones do you need to develop due to your changing landscape?* The answer isn't either/or. The answer is both. In sum, customer focus isn't about a new culture as much as it's about molding a culture that can adapt to the environment around it.

Even if you are on the right track, you'll get run over if you just sit there.

—Will Rogers

Some organizations have a difficult time adapting to changes in their environment. That is, their capacity for change isn't strong. As a result, those organizations need a much more deliberate, structured approach to ensure change happens successfully. They have to be very diligent and persistent in the change management practices we described above.

To help organizations plan and prepare for the stages of their journey, we find it helpful to get them to think about the way their organization typically approaches change. To do that, we use three categories to denote their capacity to change, and define those categories as follows:

Reactive Change: The organization is good at adjusting, responding, or adapting to change created by forces outside of the organization—customers, competitors, new technologies, emerging markets, and so forth—and is usually successful at avoiding or minimizing any fallout or damage as a result of change.

Proactive Change: The organization doesn't wait for changes to occur before responding to them, but proactively works to anticipate, prepare for, and effectively manage those changes instead of being managed by them (i.e., it acts instead of reacts).

Competitive Change: The organization creates or serves as the initiating source of change or accelerates the rate of change in an already changing situation; it leverages change as a competitive weapon to catch the competition off-guard and/or keep them in a catch-up mode.

In addition to an organization's capacity for change, the degree of change required will vary significantly from organization to organization, and will vary over time for any given organization. In our work with suppliers, we help them understand the three different levels or types of change experts typically recognize, and our particular definitions of them:

Incremental Change: reflects noticeable change or progress; fine-tunes your existing model or approach; is relatively easy to achieve; and has some degree of impact internally and externally.

Substantial Change: reflects considerable change or progress; clearly alters your existing model or approach; is moderately difficult to achieve; has significant impact inside and outside.

Transformational Change: reflects breakthrough change or progress; radically alters or replaces an existing model or approach; may be quite difficult to achieve; changes the game.

Graphically portraying where a company is in both its capacity for change and level of change can help people think about the level of effort they must expend and how closely they need to manage the change process for their journey. (See Figure 9.3.)

The level of effort an organization must expend on their change process, and the degree of managing they must apply to that process, will depend in large part on their capacity for change and the level of change they are pursuing. As an organization moves from incremental to substantial change, or from substantial to transformational change, it usually encounters increasing levels of intentional and/or unintentional internal resistance. Thus, as the level

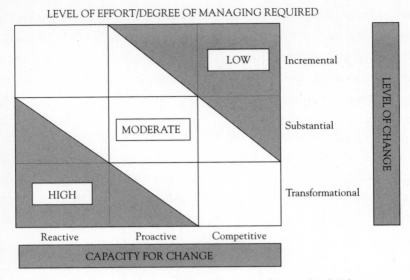

LEVEL OF EFFORT/DEGREE OF MANAGING REQUIRED

Figure 9.3   Assessing Capacity and Level of Change

of change increases, so does the amount of effort and time that's needed to generate broad-based acceptance of, then support for, and ultimately, involvement with, that change.

As a company's capacity for change evolves or matures from reactive to proactive, and from proactive to competitive, it becomes relatively easier to continually get people rallied around and dedicated to various change efforts. Conversely, the more reactive an organization's change capacity is, the harder it will have to work to change effectively. A good example of a reactive capacity for change is an organization confronted with a burning-platform situation. In essence, they need to change just to survive or stay in the game. It's a circling of the wagons where everyone digs in, gets focused, and does whatever it takes—because there is no acceptable alternative. Reactive capacity is relatively easy to get started and kicked into action, but it eventually fades in the absence of additional fires or significant change management support.

The reacting capacity for change isn't a self-sustaining, inherent capability, but is more of an episodic capability that rises in extreme cases, almost on an "as-needed" basis. It does not, however, become part of the culture. Reactive change also isn't very gratifying since the organization did a great deal of work just to "catch up." Oftentimes, there's not much to show for their efforts in terms of net gains. Lastly, people tend to believe such efforts have an endpoint as opposed to being a perpetual state or capability. The typical sentiment is: *once this is over (i.e., once the fire is out), things should return to normal.*

So reactive change cultures require a high level of effort or closely managed change activities to succeed at most change challenges— even challenges that only call for incremental change. They also require substantial effort to sustain any kind of change capability, and get an organization ready to rise again in the face of the next threat or crisis.

> *Change must become the norm, not cause for alarm.*
> —*Tom Peters, from his book* Thriving on Chaos

At the other end of the spectrum, a competitive capacity is where change *is* the normal state. Organizations with a competitive capacity for change don't think about putting fires out—they think about starting them. They drive changes that start fires burning on the competition's platform. That competitive drive can be fed for a long period of time, with relatively less effort, as the organization develops a strong sense of and commitment to keeping the competition behind them.

Such competitive changes usually generate a sense of progress or success that galvanizes an organization's competitive change culture and gives people cause for celebration. Things like new product or service launches, press releases, stock market rallies, new facility openings, competing companies going out of business, winning those "whale" accounts, sales rallies, and other successes tend to keep people alert and hungry for that next big idea or opportunity to leverage change.

Even when confronted with the need or opportunity for transformational change, the competitive change culture is much better equipped to tackle the challenge because they have so many sup-porting practices and tools already in place. Change has become not only a competitive weapon, it has become a way of life. Apple, Nike, 3M, Gillette, Amazon, and Microsoft are all good examples of com-panies that we view as having a competitive capacity for change.

Key Performance Management Practices

Managing performance is the second key area required for a customer-focused internal management system, one of the integral elements of achieving a Level III customer focus. (See Figure 9.4.)

A tool that we have used successfully for managing performance in dozens of different organizations is our driving peak perfor-mance tool. While there are countless theories and viewpoints around what separates desired performance from undesired perfor-mance, it all boils down to this: *When a person doesn't perform as desired, the cause is clarity, skill, will, or support.*

More specifically, when an individual or team doesn't perform as well as its members want, or as well as you want, it will always be due to the members' lack of one or more of these four performance drivers:

Clarity: Your performers have a clear picture of what you expect of them (goals), how your expectations are measured, and how

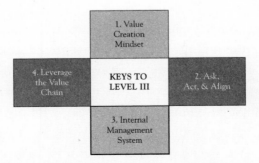

Figure 9.4   Managing Performance: Part of Your Internal Management System

those expectations impact the organization's performance and success as well as their own.

Skill: While performers might know what you expect, they also need the skill (knowledge, competency, and ability) to achieve it. Skill comes from the appropriate blend of training, coaching, modeling, and on-the-job practice.

Will (also referred to as *consequences*): When individuals are clear about what you expect and they have the ability to do it, they next must have the will to or "want" to do it. You must provide the appropriate consequences needed to shape their will, behavior, and results.

Support: Even if clarity, skill, and will exist, performers may still have obstacles that prevent their success. Helping them diagnose performance obstacles and access needed information or resources, and giving them ample authority, is also key to their success.

We'll look at each one of these a bit more closely. As you'll see, these four drivers have already come up in various other contexts throughout this book. In Figure 9.5 we pull them all together into an integrated model you can use as a management tool. We'll discuss the first three (clarity, skill, and will) below, and pick up our discussion of the fourth driver, support, a bit later in this chapter.

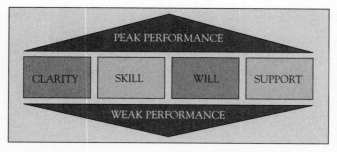

Figure 9.5   Four Drivers of Performance

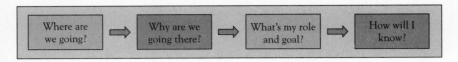

Figure 9.6   Performance Questions Related to Clarity

Clarity: "Before I know what to do, I need to know what you want or expect of me."

Clarity means your performers have a clear picture of where the organization, business, department, and/or team are going and why. They have well-defined goals that are needed to get them there, and they know in very clear terms their personal role in achieving those goals. They also can readily see where they and the team stand in terms of progress made against those goals. Annual performance goals and scorecards, customer focus or customer experience dashboards, customer relations management (CRM) reports and analyses, voice of the customer (VOC) reports and analyses, as well as broader business and financial plans and reports, are all useful tools for ensuring the clarity your performers need. Clarity provides the answers to the performance questions shown in Figure 9.6.

Skill: "I understand what you expect of me, but I need the ability to do it."

Skill includes the knowledge, competency, or ability your performers need to achieve their goals. The skills they need for their customer-focused responsibilities must come from formal training and informal on-the-job training and practice, but must be reinforced by role modeling and coaching from their managers. One tactic we see missing in so many organizations is ample opportunity for people to practice their new skills and have those dry runs observed and critiqued by their peers. Most organizations (and people) hate the idea of practice or role-playing exercises. But those who use such opportunities have the results to show for it. Skill provides the answers to the performance questions shown in Figure 9.7.

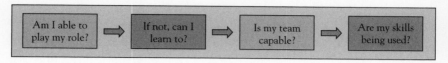

Figure 9.7   Performance Questions Related to Skill

Will: "I know what you want and I'm able to do it, but I must want to do it."

Will, also referred to as consequences, includes techniques that create a motivational or emotional connection between performers and their role and provide both positive and negative consequences for performers' behaviors and results. Will provides the answers to the performance questions shown in Figure 9.8.

While the techniques used and actions taken to create consequences are many and vary widely, the most common types of positive consequences we see used in customer focus efforts are:

- Financial incentives
- Nonfinancial rewards
- Customer and employee-nominated awards programs
- Special recognition honors and events
- Internal competitions and contests

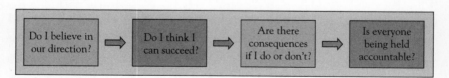

Figure 9.8   Four Performance Questions Related to Will

10-Point Customer Focus Framework

#9. Consequences

Financial Consequences

Group incentive or bonus programs are the most prevalent approach we see. In these situations, everyone in the organization receives the same financial award, provided the organization as a whole achieves its pre-set customer focus targets or goals. The goals are typically set in any number of the various economic or quantitative indicators we discussed in Chapter 2. The financial reward most often provided is a cash bonus that equals a fixed percent of their annual pay, or a fixed amount of dollar payout. For example, where organization XYZ Inc. achieves the customer focus goal they had set for the year, everyone would get a customer focus bonus or incentive payment equal to 5 percent of their annual salary or wages, or everyone might receive a flat amount of $3,000 (percentages and amounts are for illustrative purposes only). Most often, customer focus performance is one of several factors used in the calculation of total bonus or incentive payouts; is typically combined with other performance factors such as operating income (OpInc), gross margin dollars (GM $), free cash flow (FCF), return on invested capital (ROIC), return on capital employed (ROCE), safety indices, and so forth.

Another practice we often see is where the organization requires certain people to set specific individual customer focus goals at the beginning of the year. Then, their individual performance against those goals is factored in to any annual pay increases or bonus/incentive payments they would receive. We prefer this approach rather than the group incentive approach described above because this approach tends to make a much clearer and direct linkage between the individual's personal effort and results, and the consequences. That is, individuals see a direct benefit of the performance they personally achieved, whereas in the group approach, everyone tends to benefit (or lose) equally regardless of the personal role they actually played in helping reach the target. The individual goal approach, however, takes more time and thought to establish on the front end, and requires more judgment and possibly tougher decisions and conversations at the individual level on the back end.

Clearly, there are many variations of each of the above approaches, as there are various pros and cons of each variation. Organizations need to weigh what they are trying to achieve, the investment they're willing to make, and their reward philosophy and culture to ensure they have an approach that works best for them.

As an example, one company we work with uses a customer experience index (CEI) to set and track a company-wide customer-focus goal. That index has several component metrics in it including customer retention rates, customer survey scores, and gross margin gains. Imagine that at the beginning of the year they set a goal to achieve a CEI improvement of 2.5 percent. The CE bonus plan for the year might be set such that if the full 2.5 percent improvement is achieved, 5 percent of the year's gross margin dollar gains are paid out in CE bonuses. If they achieve between 2.0 percent and 2.49 percent CEI improvement, 3.5 percent of the year's gross margin dollar gains are paid out in CE bonuses. If they achieve between a 1.75 percent and 1.99 percent CEI improvement, 2.0 percent of the year's gross margin dollar gains are paid out in CE bonuses. Any CEI improvement less than 1.75 percent does not generate any CE bonuses.

In another company, each member of the senior management team member has to set a specific customer focus goal for the year that they are personally held responsible for achieving as part of their other annual performance goals. That goal might pertain to improving a certain customer focus metric, working to improve a particular customer-facing process, or leading a specific customer-focus–related joint project or cross-functional project. Whatever the goal, all members of the management team must have one, and their merit and bonus awards at the end of year are determined by the level of progress they make in achieving their respective customer focus goals.

What is most effective about this approach is that all members of the senior team, regardless of their functional role, take ownership for some aspect of the organization's customer focus. That goes a long way to create the internal alignment we talked about earlier. Of course, you gain an added benefit of that practice when each senior manager, in turn, cascades his or her customer-focus–related goal down into the rest of the organization—similarly holding the members accountable for doing their part to achieve the goal. That cascading is where the alignment and shared sense of ownership gets multiplied, and really starts becoming embedded in the organization.

The commitment to customer focus at W.W. Grainger, for example, hinges on Grainger providing a very simple incentive for employees to work hard: More success means more money in the company's profit-sharing trust, which is divided among employees every year. In 2009, for instance, the company provided $119 million to employees, which amounted to 18 percent of pay for employees with five or more years of experience.[1]

Well known provider of insurance, investment, and retirement services to military personnel and veterans, USAA (United Services Automobile Association) provides a reward/culture framework that emphasizes account growth over new account development. This sends a clear message that serving, retaining, and growing the business with current customers (clients) is more important than attracting and winning new customers. That kind of message can play a vital role in providing employees with a clear sense of priorities and an alignment around those priorities.[2]

When IBM transformed itself into a customer-centered company, the employees had to be convinced it was necessary; they had to "get it." Some of the actions IBM took to enable that included ranking and rating employees on their individual performance and their team contributions toward specific customer-focused objectives. Executive compensation, which had been based primarily on business unit performance, was now based on overall business results and customer satisfaction.[3]

---

[1] Jared Shelley, "Time to Re-Engage," *Human Resource Executive* (December 2010): cover story and page 14.

[2] Ronald Henkoff, "Growing Your Company: Five Ways to Do it Right," *Fortune*, November 25, 1996.

[3] Harvey Thompson, *Customer-Centered Enterprise* (New York: McGraw-Hill, 1999).

Recall the Kansas City Harley-Davidson plant we discussed back in Chapter 8. One need not walk very far into that facility before seeing or hearing obvious signs of how they build consequences into their culture. Every employee in the plant is on some type of variable pay plan that links individual, team, and plant performance. With few exceptions, every employee learns every job in the plant. Employees rotate to a different job every two hours. The workers are organized into self-directed work teams. Each team has its own scoreboard, which might track any number of things, even cash flow. If a team performs better than its budget, the team gets to decide what to do with the remaining cash. One team used it to hire an on-site masseuse!

There's reserved parking for owners—Harley bike owners. If you drive your Harley to work, you get to park right in front of the facility's main doors. If you drive another brand of bike to work, you park it . . . elsewhere. A super-relaxed dress code coexists with strict rules around shop-floor hygiene and safety. For example, the paint facility has strict rules about what the team can wear and eat, as well as the soap and shampoo they can use. Some foods and soaps can create skin oils that contaminate certain finishes. At several workstations, employees listen to music as they work.

As you can see, Harley-Davidson uses a blend of consequences to keep their employees aligned, engaged, and focused on their priorities. Some are financial consequences, whereas others are not.[4]

Nonfinancial Consequences

The types of nonfinancial awards, and the various mechanisms for delivering them, are even more numerous and varied than the financial ones we just discussed. In fact, the possibilities are limited

---

[4] Kansas City Harley-Davidson plant tour and meetings with work teams, May 2003, in conjunction with the annual Customer-Supplier Division Conference for the American Society of Quality.

only by the organization's imagination. We will highlight just a few examples here to give you a flavor for the range of things that are possible. In-kind awards such as fitness club memberships, gift cards, award trips, and other perks are common examples. Public award ceremonies, recognition dinners, press announcements, desktop and wall plaques, and awards are other examples. Contests and competitions can be particularly effective at generating at least awareness, if not interest, from the broader organization as a whole. Such contests can be for any number of customer-focus–related actions or results including:

- Going above and beyond to solve a customer's problem or fill a need
- Ideas for improving specific internal or customer-facing processes
- Suggestions for making internal policies more customer-friendly
- New product or service innovation ideas
- VOC score improvements by region, by product line, by business unit, and so forth

A number of companies proudly display their award winners (photos, stories, etc.) on their lobby walls, throughout their main hallways, in trophy and award cases, or on what some call their Wall of Fame. At one company, for each quarterly period, an employee is nominated by both fellow employees and customers as one of the year's four CE Champions of the Year. On the award wall is a picture of the award winner and their family members, the amount of their award,[5] detailed examples (stories) of what they did to earn the award, and testimonials from the coworkers and customers who nominated them.

---

[5] Note that this particular organization includes a cash award of $2,500, $5,000, or $10,000 depending on the type of achievements that earned someone the champion's nomination. Nevertheless, we are using their program here as an example of the nonfinancial recognition mechanisms some organizations use.

They are in the process of enhancing their Wall of Fame by using video testimonials instead of written ones wherever possible. You'll simply click the button under the CE Champion's photo, and a video will play describing his or her accomplishments and showing the coworkers and customers actually stating their testimonials. The video might also contain sound bites from the champion's family members. At the end of the year, the CEO takes all four of the nominated champions, along with their individual spouses or guests, to dinner at an exclusive area restaurant.

Negative Consequences

Providing negative consequences is just as important as, if not more important than, providing the positive ones. Unfortunately, a large majority of organizations have a difficult time making the tough decisions, and having the tough conversations, that come with creating negative consequences. This difficulty is true in any of their organizational endeavors, not just their customer focus journey. We say it's more important than the positive consequences because you can still make substantial progress if less than 100 percent of your people are aligned with and bought into your customer focus. Not everybody can be, will be, or has to be a champion for it to succeed. However, even a handful of internal resistors—depending on who they are and what job they are in—can have a noticeable diluting impact on your efforts. If some of your employees don't want to jump on the wagon of support—that's something you can probably deal with. If some of them stand in the way of that wagon—that's something you cannot tolerate.

In effect, your message and actions must persistently show people there are benefits to them for supporting the customer focus, and there are negative outcomes for those who resist or try to undermine that focus. There's no room in your organization for the latter. Such people—assuming you've been clear about your expectations and their opportunities to be supportive—need to be dealt with forthrightly and effectively. That might mean excluding them from the financial and nonfinancial incentives described earlier, taking away certain privileges or discretionary benefits, loss of potential earnings, and other penalties—up to and including moving them out of the organization. This tough talk might sound harsh or extreme, but we have seen too many situations where a small number of very vocal and influential naysayers have caused an otherwise effective customer focus to stall, decline, or just not reach its potential.

We're not suggesting you take these negative consequence actions lightly or execute them rashly. Clearly, they must be done in a reasonable and legally compliant manner. At the end of the day, however, the gains at stake in your customer focus effort are just too significant to turn a blind eye on the chronic resistors. They either need to get on the wagon or out of the barn altogether.

In the section above we discussed how will is about motivating and holding people accountable for achieving your expectations, and being willing to make tough decisions when they do or don't deliver as expected. Now we're ready to talk about the fourth driver of performance.

Support: "I know what you want, can do it, and want to, but something's stopping me."

Support is the final enabler your performers need to optimize their success. Support can come in the form of providing your performers with the right amount of needed guidance, resources, and information. Relevant competitive intelligence, customer satisfaction and loyalty data, and tools for shifting brand preference and describing your UVP are all examples of valuable support. Support might come by way of providing performers with decision-making authority and parameters, and help in problem solving and priority setting. The Value Driver Priority Matrix tool described in Chapter 7 is one example of providing the prioritization support they might need.

Performers also need periodic help in diagnosing stalled projects or assignments, getting around obstacles they can't control,

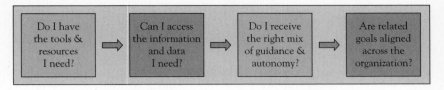

Figure 9.9   Four Performance Questions Related to Support

and evaluating and managing other types of internal interference, including lack of cooperation from other departments. Support is especially important for an organization's customer focus. To the extent some function or leader is appointed to lead an organization's customer focus charge, it is unlikely that they'll have authority over everyone who must play a direct role in the effort. As such, they will need a level of cooperation and coordination from others that can make the role quite exhausting and frustrating. Although the customer focus leader has the clarity, skill, and will, they will likely need a steady stream of support—especially early on—from executive leaders to clear internal obstacles and ensure goals and accountability are shared throughout the organization. Support provides the answers to the performance questions shown in Figure 9.9.

The Peak Performance tool can be quite valuable in terms of helping you anticipate and plan for the kind of performance effort a customer focus activity will entail. It can also be an equally valuable tool in troubleshooting and breaking through stalled efforts or related performance shortfalls or breakdowns.

Key Talent Management Practices

Talent Management is the third key area required for a customer-focused internal management system (Figure 9.10). In essence, an organization's talent management system includes all the processes, practices, tools, and policies an organization uses to manage the acquisition, retention, development, and exit of its talent or people.

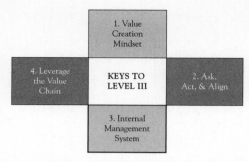

Figure 9.10   Managing Talent: Part of Your Internal Management System

Recall the customer experience pivot points described in Chapter 7 and how they represent the key points where the customer's experience or the supplier's focus significantly shifts, or pivots, between key processes, functions, or steps. A very similar principle and parallel set of processes pertain to your people and how you manage them into and through your organization. Each talent management pivot point is an opportunity to further support and enable the alignment and implementation of your customer focus. Figure 9.11 shows the talent management life cycle (also referred to as the employee's experience by some people) and its related talent management pivot points.

In most organizations, the people who are continually reviewing, improving, responding to, and leveraging the organization's customer focus are very different from the people who are designing, reviewing, improving, and leveraging the organization's people practices. Not only are these functions performed in totally separate parts of the organization, it's amazing how little they typically talk

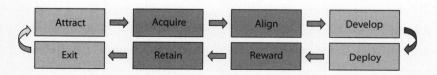

Figure 9.11   Talent Management Cycle

to each other, share information of common interest, and discuss the best way to link and mutually leverage their respective areas. In essence, customer focus people and human resources (HR) people don't collaborate or coordinate nearly enough . . . if at all.

Every step or process in the talent management cycle represents an opportunity to build or improve the organization's customer focus capabilities, effectiveness, and culture.

We've already discussed some of these linkages in other chapters, but will take a moment here to refresh and pull them all together. It begins with the type of people you're trying to *attract* and *acquire* (hire) into your organization. At Dell, for example, we believed that if we hired the right people into sales and customer care positions, we could teach them the business model, product specs and features, and any technology developments they needed to know. So we hired for the qualities we couldn't readily teach once a person was hired. Such qualities included being a self-starter and a quick study, having a natural curiosity about how people use their PC's and similar products, and having a customer-focused attitude and desire to help.

The *alignment* step begins with the employee's first day of work, and for some progressive organizations—even before that first day of work. Alignment consists of the steps an organization takes to on-board their new employees and acclimate them to the organization's culture and direction. When done well, an on-boarding process reinforces the new employee's decision to join the organization and begins building a sense of pride, connection, and brand advocacy in their new organization. When done well, this critical alignment step will tell the employee which things are somewhat important and which ones are critically important in the organization's view. In sum, the employee's early weeks on the job are an important step to ensuring they have the customer focus you want—right out of the gate. Alignment also includes the process you use for setting goals, monitoring, adjusting, and evaluating employee performance against your expectations. We've already talked about the customer focus importance of that in the performance management practices discussion.

You might note a striking parallel by now between many of the actions we suggest for creating loyal customers and the actions we're describing here for managing your talent. The above discussion on alignment is a great example. Reinforcing an employee's decision (or customer's decision) to join you (or buy from you), using the relationship to advance your brand (through employees and through customers), establishing clear expectations and goals for the relationship (with employees and with customers) are all examples of practices that are as important to your talent on the inside as they are to your customers on the outside. And there are many other parallels you might see in the areas of attracting and acquiring, as well as developing, retaining, and exiting, which are further discussed below.

Development and *deployment* are the steps and actions you take with employees once they are fully on board and performing as expected. The key here is to ensure that they not only have the clarity about what you expect, but they increasingly have the skill to deliver what you expect. That means *developing* them with the training, coaching, counseling, and assigning them to projects that develop their customer focus skills. Skill development was discussed earlier in Chapter 6.

Deploying is largely related to the consequences we discussed earlier. Are you providing the plum assignments to your customer focus champions or do the better assignments and opportunities sometimes go to your customer focus cynics? When you make promotion decisions, to what extent does the promotion candidate's customer focus commitment and results come into play? Can someone be promoted in your organization if they don't visibly and credibly support your focus? Is your succession plan populated with successors who will sustain and advance your customer focus, or is it populated with successors who will scrap it as soon as they are "in control"? In sum, if customer focus is truly important to an organization,

it should be an obvious driver in the organization's talent development and deployment activities and decisions.

Reward, *retain*, and *exit* are all part of the consequences tools or
mechanisms we discussed earlier. It's often said that you get what
you pay for. Like it or not, it's often the reality. *Rewards*, or the
withholding of rewards, can play a significant role in driving your
customer focus, as we've already discussed. Granted, many like to
think that most people will naturally do the right thing without
requiring a financial kicker to do so. But until your culture is one
in which the customer's experience is truly viewed as *everyone's* job,
that noble sentiment of people naturally doing the right thing will
be hard to make real throughout the organization.

We have had some senior leaders tell us: *I am not going to pay
someone an incentive or give them an award for something they should
already be doing as part of their job anyhow.* While we don't disagree
with the logic of that position, we don't think it's very practical. If
you expect people to automatically "get it" and support it, we sus-
pect you won't get very far—especially if you are pursuing significant
levels of change or improvement and your organization's capacity
for change is limited. In that case, people will give you lip service,
do as little as they can to comply, and try to outlast you. In such
slow-to-adapt cultures, rewards can play a vital role in kick-starting
your focus, expanding your base of champions, and getting some of
the needed customer focus processes and improvements under way.
Rewards can create early traction for your customer focus.

Please note that we're not suggesting rewards be a permanent
part of your customer focus. They will, however, be hard to avoid
in the initial stages. In time, once the culture has accepted and
learned how to use its new skills and approach, you can start making rewards less of a key part of your effort. We do, however, advise
against completely eliminating all customer-focused incentives or
awards. Most successful Level II and Level III organizations continue providing some type of opportunities for employees to earn
more as the customer focus produces more financial gains for the

organization. That is, they continue creating ways for everyone to share in the financial success customer loyalty brings.

Retain and *exit* represent another striking parallel between your customer focus and talent management efforts—and that parallel is segmentation. We discussed the importance of customer segmentation earlier. Employee segmentation is similarly very important. All employees have equal rights, but they do not have equal skills and potential. There are high potential employees—those who can significantly increase their scope and level of responsibility and contribution to the organization. There are top performers who, although they might not have as much advancement potential as high potentials, are still among your most productive or talented workers. Then there are your solid contributors—people who aren't or may never among your "A" players, but nonetheless are consistently solid performers and valued members of the team. All of these types or segments of employees are essential for your organization's success. Retaining them is critically important, and what it takes to attract, develop, and retain them often differs segment by segment.

Conversely, any organization has employee segments at the other end of the spectrum. They include people who don't currently have sufficient skills to perform as needed, but might be able to develop those skills in time. There are others who simply are not suited for the job you hired or promoted them into. Finding another job in the organization where they can succeed might be the best option for people in that segment. If other more suitable jobs don't exist, you might have to exit them from the organization. Still others have the job skills they need but just aren't the right cultural or behavioral fit for the organization. Coaching and development might help these employees in time, but in some situations, they too will need to leave the organization. Finally, and unavoidably, there will always be some number of employees who are your performance and/or behavior problem people. They either can't or won't meet your expectations—no matter what you try. They too will likely have to exit either voluntarily or involuntarily.

Please note that this retain-and-exit discussion is not meant to be a technical, human resource–related, or legal discussion of employee segments and what to do with them. Rather, we point it out to show that your employees are all different, and their value to and impact on the organization and its customers will differ. As a result, the decisions you make about retaining and exiting them will differ as well.

All of these talent management practices act to continually shape and support an organization's culture. As a result of your practices and decisions at these talent pivot points, in time, people clearly understand the kind of people the organization wants. They see it in everything you do—every hire and fire you make, every time you promote or reward someone, the people you invest in developing and those you don't, those you'll put on key projects and those you won't. Every decision you make about your people will help define and reinforce the message of what's important to the organization.

When these talent management processes are aligned with your change management and performance management processes—they form a highly effective internal management system. That's the kind of internal management system you need to drive, support, and sustain your customer focus over time. This management system is vital for preserving the gains you made in Level I and Level II and preventing any loss of traction or backsliding. It's vital to building internal core capabilities around these processes and related activities so you can eventually inspire, teach, and guide others—outside of your company—to make the same progress in their respective organizations.

Given the above discussion, we hope it's clear that a sound internal management system is critical to reaching and sustaining Level II of the customer focus journey. An organization's capability to effectively manage change, performance, and talent are all essential processes in that management system. You will not be positioned to successfully transition to and progress in Level III until those processes are developed with a customer-centric intent and are working in concert with each other and with your broader customer focus.

10-Point Customer Focus Framework

#10. Committed Leadership

One other important conclusion we hope was obvious, though not explicitly discussed above, is the need for committed leadership to provide the direction, drive, and inspiration that ensures all of this happens. It requires a leader who can create a compelling view of why a customer focus is necessary and how everyone can contribute to and benefit from it. It requires a leader who consistently and visibly demonstrates the core principles of the customer focus in their daily actions and decisions. Finally, it requires a leader who is committed to putting the customer focus first among the organization's myriad priorities. We like to test that commitment as early as possible in our work with senior leaders who are looking to take their customer focus to the next level. We typically do that by using the following three questions as our litmus test on them:

1. What outcomes are you looking to achieve with this? (Define what success looks like.)
2. Do you see this as a program or a process? (Please explain your reasoning.)
3. How willing are you to fire people to ensure it is successful?

With these questions we're trying to gauge what their own measure or proof of success is, how realistic their expectations are in terms of outcomes and timeline, and how ready they are to make tough decisions to support this.

Throughout these nine chapters, we've talked often about the many implications of those three questions. We've also talked about dozens of other perspectives, approaches, and tools that cannot be implemented in any meaningful way without the right leadership. Before leaving this internal management system discussion, let's highlight a few remaining requirements for an organization's customer-focused leadership. No matter how informed or "ready" senior leaders are to forge ahead on a customer focus journey, they are still senior leaders—many of whom still have recurring blind spots they must stay alert for and see through. Below are five of the more nagging or persistent blind spots we most often have to coach senior leaders through.

1. Once a strategy is set, the best leader's work is not done, it has just begun. You must realize leadership execution is a full-time job. Don't underestimate the level of personal effort it'll require of you, and don't overestimate how much momentum this will get without your continual personal involvement. Be ready to persistently and maniacally act as a coach, player, and cheerleader.

2. Remember that this is a marathon, not a sprint. This is not something you do when things slow down or when a crisis is upon you. It's not something you can turn on and off as needed. Since you never know where that next competitive threat or disruptive technology will come from, it must always be on. Be in this for the long haul, or don't get into it at all.

3. Don't get so consumed with macro metrics that you're missing the micro movements. CSM and other customer-centric metrics move very incrementally and do so over time. Improving CSM from 3.80 to 3.95 on a 5-point scale may seem insignificant, but you may actually be making significant progress and achievements at specific customers and individual touch points that shouldn't be discounted or ignored.

4. Resist the quick-fix syndrome. At every decision crossroad, try to find the solution that's most sustainable and that creates the most unique value for the most customer segments. Be willing to absorb some short-term pain or invest some temporary

resources if it means arriving at a longer-term, broader-scale solution or advantage.

5. Employees are influenced by what leaders do, not by what leaders say. They watch their managers much more closely than most people think they do. You and your leadership team must say what you're going to do, and then do it. Few things are more toxic to a customer focus than talking tough but not making the tough decisions that support that talk.

One Leader's Approach to Change

We saw this change-management challenge play out from start to finish working with a sleepy division of a large company. When the incumbent division president retired, the parent company chose the number two leader from another division (which was a flagship operation), and promoted him to the president of this sleepy division. In truth, he was brought in to turn it around. He spent his first 60 days meeting individually with every employee and manager in the division, as well as a cross section of various customers and suppliers. He listened much more than he talked. A quiet type, everyone thought at first. Then near the end of his second month, he called an "all hands" meeting to share what he had learned and specifically share his priorities and next steps for the year.

He began by saying he saw and heard many things he liked and was excited about. He added that he also saw and heard many things he didn't like, and they would have to change. Some of those changes (which he then described) would come in the next 90 days, and some (which he also described) would take a bit longer—but all would be complete by year's end. Then he moved to his specific priorities for the year and gave the highlights of his implementation plan, including key measures for both the near term and further out.

He finished that discussion by saying he suspected the people would view those priorities as incredibly ambitious. He further speculated that some people would view them as so ambitious that they won't want to tackle them. Then he said: "I know many of you won't like or agree with where this organization needs to get to. And that's OK. I fully expect some of you will question whether or not this will still be the right place for you. And that's OK too. Finally, I expect some of you will decide you don't want to stay. And once again, I'm OK with that." Then he paused for a full minute—as he looked around the large room and tried to make quick eye contact with every person there.

Finally he said, "If I'm not sure about you being able or willing to change and grow with us, I'll be meeting with you over the next 30 days to discuss that with you. If you're not sure about your desire or ability to be part of where we're going, I'm happy to meet with you. If you are ready to invest yourself fully into this year of intense challenge—I promise you'll reap the benefits—if we succeed."

This "state of the future" presentation, which some employees later called it, effectively set the stage for a series of changes that this organization would end up making, successfully, over the ensuing two years. When we asked various employees there what they felt made it as successful as it was, they cited several factors including these:

- When he (the new president) committed to doing something—he delivered on that commitment.
- He worked tirelessly to meet every employee in the division and spent time in small groups, as well as one-on-one meetings—over coffee, over a sandwich, during a truck driver's route, or on a salesman's call to an account.

(continued)

- Within six months, he had assembled a small but highly engaged team of change champions that cut across the entire organization and included people at various levels—top to bottom.

- Within nine months, he had promoted one key player, moved two other senior leaders into positions of lesser responsibility (no title changes, but clearly demotions), and two other senior managers elected to leave the organization to "pursue other opportunities."

- He assigned a change-related performance goal to every department head and made those goals account for 50 percent of their year-end bonus calculations.

- He told people: "If you're willing to speak your mind, and use your mind to speak, I *will* listen." And according to the employees, that's exactly what he did.

In conclusion, Level III is a level where the organization's customer focus and its culture are completely linked, integrated, and indistinguishable from one another—the two are one in the same. The customer focus is a business priority that permeates and defines the culture. The culture of the organization is customer focused.

That sameness becomes evident in the way the employees talk, think, and behave. It's clear in their realization of why their company exists, and the role customer value plays in that existence. It's clear in their understanding of how the company makes money, the role the customer's experience plays in them making that money, and the role they play in that customer experience. It's an alignment of purpose and focus that gives every employee the permission, and an obligation, to think like the customer, challenge each other to think that way, and act in ways that differentiate the company in the customer's eyes.

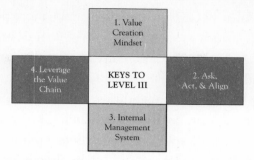

Figure 9.12   Three of the Keys to Level III

Finally, it's a culture made possible and reinforced by an integrated internal approach to managing change, performance, and talent. In sum, Level III is where your customer focus has been articulated, reinforced, rewarded, and driven in every function, department, and aspect of your business. (See Figure 9.12.)

Level III is also the level where the processes you improved, the new skills you learned, the new systems you established, and the new touch point relationships you capitalized on are no longer *new*. They're no longer experiments you're trying or methods you're practicing. They have become real capabilities within your organization, which you consistently execute. They are no longer the priority of your customer service and support teams, or of your sales and marketing personnel. They have become the overarching priority or focus of *everyone* in your organization. The ability to identify, articulate, and deliver unique customer value that truly differentiates your company is no longer limited to your sales transactions or your products and service. You now have people positioned throughout the entire customer experience who know how and are motivated to create that differentiation. Differentiation has become a core capability.

As a result of your continually improving capabilities and evolving culture, you have created meaningful barriers to entry and other competitive advantages that have translated into any number of economic gains including: new revenue streams; higher margins;

lower costs of sales; cycle time improvements; more productive and collaborative relationships; greater share of your customers' wallets; repeat and referral business; and many of the other economic gains we've discussed.

When people use the capabilities and advantages like those above in describing your organization, you'll know you have arrived at Level III in terms of your customer focus maturity. If that were the end of your journey, you would likely already be way ahead of any competitor in your space. Your economic growth would be light years ahead of where you were before you started the journey. Indeed, you would have come a long, long way! However, as we've often said, this journey has no end. Even at the enviable level described above, there are still untapped possibilities for further optimizing your progress—ways to yet extend and further leverage your capabilities and culture. Our next chapter discusses this fourth key element of Level III—further leveraging your value-creating culture across your broader value chain.

CHAPTER 10

Leveraging Your Culture and Value Chain

- Leverage your existing customer and employee loyalty
- Increase your teaming and elevate it to partnering
- Extend Level III practices to the broader value chain

To recap and connect our various discussions thus far, Level I customer focus (A) revolved around voice of the customer (VOC) activities and sought to measure, track, and improve the supplier's ability to identify, or detect, and meet the customer's unmet needs at the point of transaction. Level II customer focus (B) concentrated on teaming with the customer in ways that further differentiated the supplier's ability to deliver value, developed a more complete view of customer value and unstated needs, and created barriers to entry at multiple touch points across the entire customer's experience. (See Figure 10.1.)

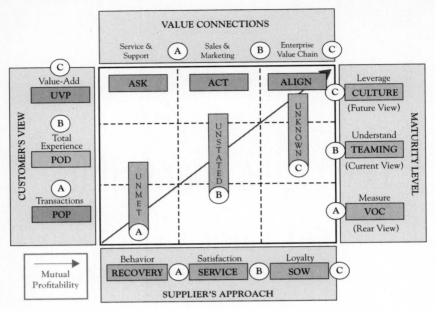

Figure 10.1   Customer Focus Maturity Model®

Level III is all about building and leveraging a customer-centric culture (C); building a culture that is characterized by an *ask*, *act*, and *align* mindset in every aspect of the supplier's business. It involves sustaining that culture with a system of internal management practices that support and drive the customer focus, and are aligned with each other. Finally, Level III is about leveraging that culture to continually improve the supplier organization's internal effectiveness, extending the loyalty of the supplier's customers and employees, and proactively engaging the rest of the supplier's value chain to surface unknown opportunities to add value and optimize the mutual profitability of Level III relationships and practices.

LEVEL III

Drive and Leverage Your Value-Creating Culture

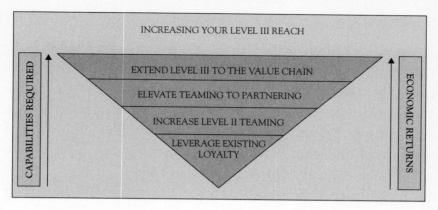

Figure 10.2   Increasing Your Level III Reach

This final chapter is about fully capitalizing on all of the capabilities and customer focus differentiators you've developed during the journey through Levels I, II, and III. It's about increasing the impact of those capabilities and taking steps to leverage your culture into other parts of your value chain. The ultimate goal is to align the key players in that chain, and optimize their relationships and interactions for the mutual benefit of everyone involved.

There are four steps Level III suppliers take over time to further extend the reach, impact, and gains of its Level III capabilities and culture. Not all Level III organizations take all four steps, but some degree of progress in each step is essential for taking full advantage of related opportunities for revenue and profit growth. Those four steps are depicted in Figure 10.2. Each step builds on the prior step below it; and each successive step involves more advanced capabilities, as well as more economic return.

Leverage Existing Loyalty

Level III organizations take active steps to leverage the existing loyalty they've generated, at all three levels, into broader brand advocacy both outside and inside of the organization. This means they take existing loyal relationships and ensure they are translating or extending into advocacy and growth for their brand.

Helping Your Customers Extend Their Loyalty

One misconception supplier organizations often have is they assume their loyal customers will automatically, or naturally, behave or act like loyal customers in all situations. For example, you might be enjoying your desired share of wallet (SOW) with a given customer, and they might clearly prefer you to other suppliers, and buy from you instead of from other suppliers. Those benefits, however, are still limited to their immediate relationship with you. Their loyalty to you has not yet extended beyond that relationship into their relationships with others. While they might give you high marks on your surveys, they might be reluctant to provide you with testimonials. While they might prefer your brand, they aren't necessarily advocating your brand to others, which is the type of leveraged loyalty you ultimately want in Level III. You gradually want more and more of your customers going out of their way to generate awareness, publicly promote your brand, and help create demand for your offerings.

Some customers will do this naturally as they become increasingly satisfied with and loyal to you. Others will not. That's why many supplier organizations have an explicit approach or process to ensure a customer's loyalty is leveraged as much as possible. (Recall that *leveraging loyalty* was actually a key pivot point in the customer's experience map in Chapter 7.) They don't assume it will happen without their prompting and driving it.

Customers often fail to take this important next step on their own either because they don't want to, or because they just haven't thought about it.

We find that some customer organizations try to avoid, or don't like to discuss the notion of being loyal to a supplier, even though their preferences and decisions are clearly that of a loyal customer. They often avoid it because they don't want other potential suppliers to be discouraged from approaching them with better deals, or they want to portray an image of spreading their spend across various suppliers—not just to their preferred ones. As a result, they are reluctant or slow to act when it comes to advocating one particular supplier. Other customers shy away from the loyalty label because they don't really understand what loyalty means. They focus too much on the word, and lose sight of the positive behaviors you're after.

For example, in one particular company, their customer satisfaction measurement (CSM) survey asked a question about how likely the customer would be to refer the supplier to others. Some responding customers who gave the supplier very high marks in all areas of the survey said they would not refer the supplier to others. The explanations they gave included such comments as:

- "Why would I let other companies know about my secret?!?!"
- "The more customers I send your way, the harder it will be to get your attention."
- "You seem awfully slow to commit additional resources as you grow. Maybe if we saw a better job of you staffing up for growth, we'd be more willing to help you grow."
- "We've got a good thing going right now—adding more players to the picture just confuses things."
- "As a matter of company policy, we do not make those kinds of referrals."

In many cases, where an otherwise loyal customer is hesitant about making a referral or providing a testimonial, it is often because they feel the supplier's attention or service to them might be diluted as the supplier is spread thinner and thinner across a growing customer base. Interestingly, in several cases where a seemingly loyal survey respondent cited company policy as the obstacle, we found that there really was not any company policy prohibiting it. The individual respondent was actually using policy as an excuse to avoid surfacing other issues that were really bothering him. Still other customers, who may or may not be willing to provide the referrals or testimonials you seek, just don't realize how important it might be to you, or just haven't thought about it . . . yet.

You can't assume a customer is going to naturally behave like a loyal customer outside of their immediate relationship with you. Oftentimes, you have to let them know that's what you need or want from them. And in some cases, you'll have to educate them about what it means and you may even have to help them script it or verbalize it in a way that both makes them comfortable and helps advance your interests and growth goals.

One final comment about this before we move on: Many supplier organizations don't do a good job of closing the loop with or recognizing their customers who have provided testimonials or referrals. That's why we like to see a supplier's process include a specific step that circles back to and thanks a customer for having made a referral, or for having provided a testimonial that was used in a successful proposal or bid situation. Granted, closing the loop with them sounds like common sense, but it's not a very common practice.

Helping Your Employees Extend Their Loyalty

Similarly, your employees won't automatically or instinctively know their role in promoting your brand unless you tell them that's what you expect and you show them how, or equip them to do so. We discussed earlier, in some detail, how the various parts of your talent management practices can support or frustrate various aspects of your customer focus. All of those practices help you attract, retain, and motivate the employees you need to fulfill your brand promise to your customers, thus improving and sustaining the loyalty of your customers. One other practice we find can be helpful in aligning your employees to your customer focus is helping everyone see a clear linkage between your external and internal brand promises (i.e., the linkage between your commercial and employer brands).

When we talk about an internal or employer brand, we mean the intellectual and emotional connection you create between your

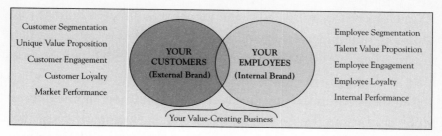

Figure 10.3   Aligning External and Internal Brands

organization and all employees (current, past, and future employees). It is the experience people expect to have as an employee of your organization. It is very similar to a commercial brand that represents, generally, the experience customers expect to have with your organization. Accordingly, both your external and internal brands depend on a number of parallel factors, as is illustrated in Figure 10.3.

For example, are you investing your time and money on the employee segments that create the most value for your organization? Do you have an employee or talent value proposition that describes what employees can expect from you and what you, in turn, expect from them? Are you engaging your employees in a way that optimizes their performance and impact on your customer's experience? Do you have a high retention rate for your high-performing employees? Do your employees advocate your organization as a place to work and encourage their friends and relatives to seek employment with you? Sound familiar? Can you see the linkage?

The importance of aligning your external and internal brands is all too often overlooked by organizations. In fact, most organizations don't even recognize the need for or possibility of an internal brand. Others, however, not only recognize it, they seek to highlight and leverage it. A recent example of this recognition was with restaurant giant McDonald's Corporation. McDonald's employee satisfaction rating had been consistently above 80 percent—a very favorable rating by most standards. However, customer views of the company's work environment consistently scored in the 30 to

40 percent range. While this disconnect was concern enough, the situation was punctuated when the word "McJob" was added to the Merriam-Webster Dictionary as "a low-paying job that requires little skill and provides little opportunity for advancement."

Realizing customers had a much lower opinion of the jobs at McDonald's than their own employees did, the company knew they needed to get the real message about employment at the company out to the public. They defined a global Employee Value Proposition that they could pass onto the public through those who knew it best—their employees. Branded as the three F's, they created and disseminated an employment brand based on an employee value proposition of Family & Friends, Flexibility, and Future. The initiative included educating employees on talking points they could use when talking to friends and customers about the quality of the company's food, service, and employment. The McDonald's story provides an excellent example of many of the customer–supplier connections and drivers we've been discussing in this book.[1]

The first step to increasing your Level III reach is to actively request, guide, and equip your loyal customers and employees to be advocates for your brand. Take specific steps that help leverage their loyalty beyond their own experience—beyond the customer's sale transaction with you and beyond the employee's hiring transaction with you—and extend their loyalty to favorably influence and attract others to your brand.

Increase Level II Teaming

Level III organizations replicate and leverage what they've learned and accomplished with an increasingly larger portion of their customer base. That is, they seek to increase, through teaming, the types and number of customers they're engaging at various levels of maturity.

---

[1] Kristen Morgan, "McDonald's—Building Reputation through a Global Employee Value Proposition," HRM Today, March 4, 2011, www.hrmtoday.com/featured-stories/mcdonald%E2%80%99s-%E2%80%93-building-reputation-through-a-global-employee-value-proposition/.

Applying Your Skills and Techniques to More Customers

We noted in Chapter 3 that launching a customer focus journey is not necessarily the same journey for every customer or customer segment. Some customer relationships are already strong enough that you might not need a VOC mechanism to help position the touch point dialogues you need to make Level II teaming advancements. It might just be a natural or logical extension of the things you're already doing with that customer. For other customers, you might have effective dialogues already under way at some touch points, but just need to replicate them at other touch points of that customer's experience. Or you might have various types of teaming going on with some of a given customer's locations or business units, but not with all of their locations or units. Then there are other customers for whom you haven't started to engage beyond your current Level I activities with them; and some you may not be engaging at all. They may be one of the customers, or in one of the customer segments, that were low on your priority target list when you were deciding which ones to focus on.

The key is that once you are comfortable that you have your priority customers or segments at the right level of focus, you should set your sights on increasing your Level II engagement or teaming with that next customer segment or group of customers. There are, however, some segments or customers that may never justify an effort from you beyond the sales transaction or perhaps beyond your VOC related activities. There are some customers where it just doesn't make sense to invest anything more because an appropriate return isn't likely to be realized.

Also note that, in time, new customers will come into the picture and you'll need to slot them into your prioritization process. Conversely, customers will leave for various reasons. They go out of business. They're bought by, or merge with, another company. They have an executive level change in control that ushers in a different (competing) vendor or a new approach or requirements for the procurement function or process. There might even be customers where you ended the relationship. Whatever the circumstances, there will be customers who leave. These additions and deletions to your customer base should cause you to periodically reevaluate your segments and related customer focus priorities.

Level III organizations continually reevaluate and reprioritize their customer focus target list and they continually widen their customer focus net so it covers an increasing number or types of customers. In essence, Level III organizations have a continual progression of customers moving into or through each level of the maturity model. The ultimate goal is to continue finding, improving, and capitalizing on those customer relationships that can be raised to Level III relationships and mutual profitability.

Applying Your Skills and Techniques Internally

There's one other dimension of this discussion about increasing the number of Level II customers that we want to point out. Before a supplier organization can be highly effective at having touch point dialogues, joint problem solving, and other forms of teaming with an increasing number of its customers, it must be effective at teaming internally. A problem we have seen suppliers frequently encounter is where one member of or function within their organization is openly critical (to the customer) of another member of or function elsewhere within the supplier organization. Situations periodically arise where supplier personnel are talking with a customer and, for example, field sales blames something on inside sales, or customer service blames something on transportation, or where manufacturing blames something on engineering, and so on.

"Throwing your colleague under the bus" can happen for any number of reasons. The customer is complaining about another part of the supplier's business and the supplier rep agrees with them just to appease them, or to try to diffuse the situation, or even to deflect the blame or problem elsewhere just to get the target off of their own back. Or the supplier rep acts like they agree with the customer's criticism because the rep wants the customer to feel that he or she is *on their side*. Or the supplier rep may actually agree with the criticism and takes the opportunity to pile on with his or her own complaints, hoping it will somehow bubble up to someone in authority who will be forced to address it. The motives can vary, but the reality is that people are human and they will often take pot shots at people or processes in their own organization when they are confronted with an angry, frustrated, or strong-minded customer.

It's because of these potential internal blame battles that we emphasized earlier the importance of training and tools to prepare the supplier's people to effectively engage in these Level II customer activities. These same internal skirmishes are one of the reasons we spend substantive time prior to our Value Chain Labs® workouts preparing the supplier team for their lab meeting with their customer.

In fact, we have seen some supplier organizations actually use the workout process internally to resolve internal issues, break down silos and align goals, and correct process or communications disconnects or bottlenecks. One particular organization made Lab-type internal workouts a mandatory feature. Any department or team in the company that wanted to improve or fix a relationship with another department or team could request a Lab with that other department or team. All Lab requests had to be honored. That is, participation was mandatory once a workout was requested by any initiating department or team.

For example, if product development requested a Lab with manufacturing—both sides were obligated to participate. If the warehouse and inventory team requested a Lab with the field services team—both sides were required to engage in the process. The CEO of this organization wanted to do everything possible to identify and resolve internal process and relationship issues before embarking on any workouts with customers.

Internal workouts conducted between different internal functions, departments, and teams are vital to this process. They might include:

- HQ and Division Personnel
- Faculty and Administration
- Line Managers and Staff Managers
- Marketing and Sales Staff
- Physicians and Nurses
- Field and Inside Sales Teams
- Regional Managers and Product Managers
- Engineering and Manufacturing Personnel
- QA Testers and Production Supervisors
- Customer Service and Account Execs
- Sales Managers and Sales Teams
- Finance and Operations Personnel
- Call Center and Accounting Teams
- Software Engineers and Desk Top Support Staff

The number of possible lab match-ups in a given organization is wide-ranging and depends on how dysfunctional, functional, or optimal the various internal relationships and connections are. In sum, Level III organizations take a number of steps to continually develop and apply their teaming skills and techniques in a way that helps extend the impact of their loyal customers and employees, and related capabilities.

Elevate Teaming to Partnering

The third step that Level III organizations take to increase their reach or impact is to go beyond the teaming of Level II and elevate it to a "partnering" relationship with a selected group of key customers.

Partnering Generates Mutual Success

Customer–supplier partnerships mean different things to different people, but for our purposes here, we view it as a shared realization that both parties have entered into their arrangement or relationship to make money. It's a mutual mindset that says: *my side wins when both sides win*. In essence, we define Level III partnering as follows:

> A business "partnership" is one in which each side is as interested in the other side's success as they are in their own success.

This level of partnership can only exist after a customer and supplier relationship has withstood the test of time, has endured various business up and down cycles together, and, as a result, they have established a mutual sense of confidence and trust. It is a feeling that develops over time that says we're both in this together, there's no problem we shouldn't be able to resolve, and there's nothing we shouldn't be able to talk about as long as it's legal and ethical.

Level III partnering can only occur when a supplier has consistently demonstrated its ability to deliver value, where the customer has been a regular advocate for the supplier, and where both organizations have demonstrated their willingness and ability to deal with tough issues and pursue mutual success. Only then will both sides be comfortable enough and interested enough to look forward together and anticipate what unknowns might be around the next corner. What might the next disruptive technology be in the customer's industry or in the supplier's industry? What trends, threats, or opportunities might be emerging in their respective markets and businesses that might have implications for both sides? What other opportunities for saving costs, increasing revenues, improving productivity, or reducing cycle time have they left untapped? Lastly, what skills and processes do they need to help them continually explore and address these questions together?

As an example, GE's Aircraft Engine Division (now called GE Aviation) made jet engines that were bought by Boeing and installed on Boeing aircraft. They had a good relationship with Boeing—and both companies wanted to win. According to a presentation made about GE's customer–supplier workouts by Dave Ulrich to

Coopers & Lybrand, GE wanted to sell, and Boeing wanted to buy, good engines. Both sides had cost pressures. During their partnering efforts, they learned that before GE shipped an engine, it had to pass a 1,000-point quality checklist. And before Boeing installed that same engine on a plane, Boeing put it through its own 1,000-point checklist. Some of those check points overlapped. Although some overlap is good, too much can be wasteful. Even if 25 percent of it could be done only once, both sides would save substantial time and money. They discovered they both could win if they managed the quality review process together.[2]

But Customers Don't Want "Partners"!

The push back we most often get from companies who are at the brink of Level III is the claim: *But our customers don't want "partners." They just want a product that meets their specs and price, gets to them on time, and is still working after our truck leaves their loading docks.* They aren't looking for their suppliers or vendors to be their partners. It's all about the transaction. They want to get what they pay for and nothing more. Deliver it, bill me, and then leave me alone unless I call you with problems. Sounds familiar, doesn't it?

As realistic and practical as that sounds, we don't believe it! Our experience shows otherwise. It's very similar to the common perception that price drives the majority of sales. When we ask customers to list the various factors that they consider before choosing a product or a supplier, price is always one of the factors. But surprisingly, price is not always the most important factor. In fact many customers can cite multiple examples where they paid a higher price because of their relationship with the seller, the value they got for the higher price, the convenience they were willing to pay more to get, and others. The point is—the customer will always tell

---

[2] Note: At the time of this presentation (1995), Dave Ulrich was providing consulting services to the senior leaders at Coopers & Lybrand.

you price is the key—but their behaviors and decisions often say otherwise.

In a similar vein, they will usually tell you they don't want a "partner," but experience says otherwise. In our consulting work, we survey, interview, or simply meet with hundreds of customers a year who buy products and services from our various clients. One of the things we frequently do in those surveys or interviews is ask them to complete this sentence:

"The added value I look for my supplier or vendor to bring to the table is . . ."

The resultant answers we get are quite telling, and while they cover a broad range of ideas, the answers we get most often are:

- "Know how we use your products and how they impact our results."
- "Bring me new ideas and opportunities for reducing my TCO [total cost of ownership]."
- "Understand my company's competitive and economic drivers."
- "Show me how to get the most value out of the products you sell me."
- "Help me anticipate and exploit new trends in my industry and products."

So while customers may say they don't want partners, they do want and value results that go beyond the transaction—results that create an added benefit unique to and for them, results they get only from their value-add suppliers. Call it partnering, call it advising, call it collaborating, educating, or just consulting—whatever you call it, it represents a real opportunity to take your customer focus, your customer's experience, and your mutual profitability to a higher level.

As we've cautioned several times before, Level III partnering is not for all of your customers, and will never be the right focus for many of them. In addition, this type of partnering takes a lot of time not only to discuss, evaluate, and work through your mutual interests, but also to maintain the open relationship or communications channels and processes you have in place to support it. You simply won't have the resources, time, and capacity to partner like this with all of your customers. But for those you do, the favorable outcomes can be substantial.

In sum, Level III is characterized by a forward-looking relationship, a shared lens into the future that requires a mutual interest so deep and transparent that both sides work together to anticipate, plan for, define, and ultimately succeed in, their future together.

Extend Level III Efforts Across the Value Chain

We talked in the second step about increasing the numbers or types of customers you are engaging in Level II activities. In this final step, we seek to replicate and leverage what you've learned and accomplished—not just at Level II, but at all three levels—with more and more of your customers, as well as with your suppliers, alliance partners, and literally any organization in your value chain. The kinds of productivity, revenue, and costs improvements a supplier organization can achieve by engaging its key customer segments can also be achieved with many other players across the supplier's entire value chain. When an organization can leverage these types of mutually beneficial encounters across their broader value chain, they can multiply the gains they make in terms of cycle time (productivity), innovative ideas (revenue streams), and efficiencies (costs), among others.

In effect, this step involves the organization using any combination of the ideas, techniques, and practices discussed at all three levels in an effort to influence and improve the effectiveness of its broader value chain. This step goes beyond organizations just trying to improve the economics and loyalty of their customer accounts. It includes organizations reaching out to their respective suppliers for similar improvements and competitive advantages.

For example, one company with whom we are currently working was recently contacted by one of their key customers who is assembling an Innovation Task Force. That customer organization is inviting selected value chain members to meet with organization members in a series of sessions and engage in environmental scanning, forward-looking thought leadership, and ideation conversations.

Level III value chain initiatives might involve the supplier organization reaching out to collaborate or work more closely with the suppliers or customers of their respective suppliers and customers. An example of this was demonstrated by United Missouri Banks (UMB).[3] UMB is a large regional bank, which, because of its size, is able to negotiate favorable pricing terms with many of its suppliers—suppliers who provide the bank with tangible products ranging from paper to furniture. UMB supplies many small local banks with a variety of financial products, as well as certain lending and back-office services. These small banks buy many of the same tangible products from the same suppliers as UMB but at higher prices.

As a result of collaborative partnering between UMB and the smaller banks, UMB created an Internet-based system through which it deals with its suppliers, and it allows its small bank customers to use the system to do the same. Everyone wins with this partnering. Suppliers are assured larger market share and do not have to issue bills directly to the small banks anymore. Instead, they send a consolidated invoice to UMB, which pays on its own behalf as well as that of the small banks. UMB then bundles the supplier charges with its other service fees to the small banks. UMB benefits

---

[3] Michael Hammer, *The Agenda: What Every Business Must Do to Dominate the Decade* (New York: Crown Business, 2001), 191.

in many ways: It receives a settlement fee for paying on behalf of the small banks; its purchasing volumes go up, and in turn its costs go down; and it holds its small bank customers even closer by providing an additional service. The small banks in turn benefit from lower prices and a simplified purchasing process.

Such value chain engagement or teaming might even include an organization collaborating with a totally unrelated player. A good example can be found in a situation that developed between General Mills and Land O'Lakes.[4] Prior to this, the two companies did not work together and were of no interest to each other. At the time, General Mills was looking to cut costs out of its supply chain, and realized that when its refrigerated trucks laden with Yoplait Yogurt left its General Mills warehouses, the trucks oftentimes were not full. Quite often, the truck was carrying yogurt destined for multiple supermarkets or grocery stores—meaning the truck would have multiple stops to make. If there were any traffic, mechanical, or receiving-related delays along the delivery route, the result could be, and often was, frustrated store managers waiting for their late yogurt deliveries.

General Mills realized it could address this problem by working with another company not in its product space—the butter and margarine maker Land O'Lakes. Instead of each company operating its own semiproductive distribution system, the two decided to operate their distribution networks together. They began storing Yoplait Yogurt and Land O'Lakes butter in the same warehouses, and transporting them in the same trucks to the same supermarkets and grocery stores. This resulted in their "shared" trucks leaving the warehouses with larger (fuller) loads. Since each truck was delivering more products to each store, it would have fewer stops to make, thus increasing the likelihood of on-time delivery. Both companies enjoyed the benefits of reduced distribution costs and more satisfied customers

[4] Hammer, *The Agenda* (2001), 190.

(i.e., the grocery store managers). It was to their mutual advantage to find ways to work together.

An interesting footnote to this example is that one of General Mills' principles regarding such business-to-business collaboration is that you can't collaborate with other companies until you can collaborate internally. Get different parts of your own company working well together first—then, you can extend the idea to outside parties.

In conclusion, the overarching purpose or objective of Level III is to use the capabilities you've developed, and the culture shaped by those capabilities, to accomplish the following objectives:

- Nurture and reinforce loyalty and brand advocacy within and outside of your organization.
- Use effective teaming skills and techniques within and outside of your organization.
- Engage in forward-looking partnering to anticipate future opportunities and threats.
- Apply the above steps not just with your customers, but also across your broader value chain.

To Summarize . . .

As we noted at the outset, an effective business strategy must first and foremost inspire your customers to act in a way that grows your business. Therefore, at the heart of any strategy that's going to succeed must be a clear and compelling plan to drive customers and potential customers to make decisions that favor you over your competitors. We hope you can now see how a customer focus can drive, sustain, and optimize the multiple decisions your current, prospective, and former customers make each day about their suppliers and potential suppliers.

Customer focus can only translate into the kind of business gains you seek if it is based on both a proven plan and the capabilities needed to effectively implement that plan. As we've shown throughout this book, there are 10 key elements required for an effective customer focus plan:

10-POINT CUSTOMER FOCUS FRAMEWORK

1. Strategic Drivers
2. Customer Segmentation
3. Customer Engagement
4. Employee Engagement
5. Training and Tools
6. Process Orientation
7. Joint Workouts
8. Capacity for Change
9. Consequences
10. Committed Leadership

The amount of success any organization will have with its customer-centric business strategy will depend on two factors: the time it takes the organization to see the value of and effectively develop and implement each of these 10 elements; and, the degree to which all 10 elements are aligned with each other and aligned with the rest of the business. We have shown you many of the reasons why each of these elements is important and the critical role they play in the organization's success. We have also spent considerable time explaining steps and techniques used to align these key elements with each other and with the rest of the business priorities, practices, and processes.

The key question is: *How long will it take a given organization to understand, implement, and align each of these elements?* The answer is infinitely varied. Each organization morphs or evolves over time as determined by the dynamics of its business model, competitive landscape, customer base, and culture. As a result, the pace of each organization's customer focus journey or maturation is different. Regardless of their unique rates of progress, most organizations embarking on a customer focus journey will travel through three main stages or maturity levels of their implementation.

Level I—Detect and correct unmet customer needs and issues

Level II—Define and deliver customer value at each touch point

Level III—Drive and leverage a value-creating culture

We use the Customer Focus Maturity Model® (CFMM) to illustrate that implementation journey. (See Figure 10.4 for the complete model.)

The model is used to portray and discuss the drivers, opportunities, and techniques needed to increasingly optimize an organization's

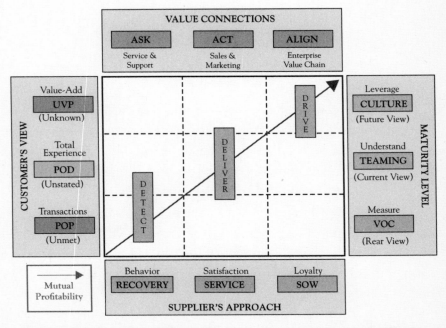

Figure 10.4   The CFMM Reaches Mature Customer Focus at Level III

customer-centric strategy by continually progressing or maturing until they reach Level III—the level that represents optimal profitability for both customer and supplier.

The ultimate goal is to advance to and through, as much as is possible and practical, a Level III customer focus. A level where your organization operates as an end-to-end process that exists for one sole purpose: to anticipate, deliver, and profit from creating customer value. A process that aligns everyone in every function, from the executive level to the entry level, from employees who face the customer to employees whose faces you never see, around that one common purpose: a culture that continually improves and connects the things going on inside your organization to the opportunities going on outside—both with your customers and your suppliers—to create a new way of viewing and leveraging your entire value chain.

INDEX